Church Music

Church Music

ILLUSION AND REALITY

Archibald T. Davison

HARVARD UNIVERSITY PRESS · CAMBRIDGE

1966

Library of Congress Catalog Card Number: 52-5393
Printed in the United States of America
Third Printing

TO

EDWARD PERRY DANIELS

Clergyman, Musician, and Idealist

May his clear understanding of the true significance of reality in church music prove to be clerically contagious.

Preface

In 1933 the author of this book issued a volume on church music, and the mere announcement of intention to write more on this subject has provoked a noticeable lifting of the eyebrows among cynical friends. This is not at all because that first book could be considered one to end all books of its kind—the author, indeed, was fully aware of its limitations—but rather because unless one deals with history, a project for which in this case the writer feels no inclination, the subject of church music is not susceptible of extended literary expansion. Worship music, these friends assure me, is in nearly all respects exactly what it was in 1933. Then why a second book? Justification lies in an unceasing and to some, it may be assumed, an apparently fanatical concern with this matter, and it would constitute a severe indictment of the sincerity of that interest had not the author in the intervening eighteen years arrived at a broader and a deeper viewpoint; one that deals more with basic causes and less with the results of individual behavior. Whatever approach be made to the subject, however, certain issues are fundamental, and though a number of these found place in the previous work they are, of necessity, recapitulated here; even a small number of quotations, seemingly unmatchable in their appropriateness, have been repeated.

The material of the present book is based on three courses of public lectures: two of them offered at the Lowell Institute in Boston in 1935 and 1940 respectively; the other, the Gates Lectures, delivered for the year 1948 at Grinnell College. The generosity of both institutions in permitting the publication of the material of these lectures is most deeply appreciated.

At this point the author would like to make his position clear in four details: First, as to what may appear to be his monotonous disagreement with certain aspects of contemporary church music material and practice. The truth is, of course, that a number of churches do live by a high musical standard as their service lists reveal, but these churches represent a lamentably small minority and it seems better to pay them homage here than to add to each adverse criticism tiresome acknowledgment that the evil is not undiluted. Second, it should not be assumed that the author is writing only of rural or small urban churches where funds for the maintenance of music are severely restricted. Among the churches whose programs of music are distinctly inferior are many supported by wealthy metropolitan congregations. Size and affluence bear no relation to quality; an inflated budget for music is, indeed, too often an invitation to rivalry with the concert hall and the opera house. Third, although some references are made to the failure of the *service* of worship to pay due respect to dignity, order, and beauty, it should be emphasized that the Roman Catholic and Protestant Episcopal churches are excluded from anything that is said in this connection. The music of both communions is by no means above reproach, but encouragement is not offered, at least, to musical superficiality as it is in services that are inchoate, egocentric, and aesthetically deficient. Fourth, the author is writing in a threefold capacity: as a musician, as an organist and choirmaster of long experience in a variety of churches, and as a layman who finds church music a distraction from rather than an incitement to worship. Whatever opinions are expressed, then, result not from prejudice or caprice but are consistently based on evidence of a technical nature and upon aesthetic and religious conviction.

It is readily conceded that there is ample room for disagreement with the writer's theories regarding church music. A sincere and intellectually convinced difference of opinion is invariably to be respected and in this case even welcomed, as it gives evidence of a "going in the tops of the mulberry trees" whose leaves are seldom stirred by the slightest breath of comment. But as to the music itself the author can, in all conscience, admit no compromise, and from those who blindly mistake prettiness for beauty, rhetoric for eloquence, commonness for devoutness, and tinsel for music's purest gold, he wholeheartedly dissents. It may seem to the reader that in its zeal for dignity and artistic worth this book is intractably professional and fantastically purist. To such an objection the author can only say that in his opinion no man to whom the God he worships is perfect with a perfection that transcends human imagining could be held sincere did he not, to the utmost, maintain toward church music the most inflexibly purist ideals reinforced by every critical faculty he possesses.

My sincere thanks are here expressed to Olin Downes, Virgil Thomson, and Daniel Pinkham, whose contributions impart a distinction to this book which it would not otherwise have. I am also indebted to Raphael Demos, of Harvard University; Holcombe Austin, of Wheaton College; and John G. Greene, of Boston; and to Charles Kletzsch, whose help in compiling the list of anthems found at the back of this book materially lightened my labors. Finally, to my wife I offer more than a simple acknowledgment of gratitude; her encouragement has been unfailing and her varied assistance invaluable.

Archibald T. Davison
Cambridge, 1951

Contents

Introduction

Any study of church music includes far more than is implied in an examination of that other branch of vocal art, the secular. The music of the world requires for its understanding mainly a knowledge of the musical material itself, though social and historical considerations must, of course, be taken into account. Church music, unlike secular music, is surrounded by a labyrinth of peripheral detail embracing not only historical and social matter but theological, psychological, and educational connections as well.[1] The story of secular music is largely the story of the products of human imagination; the story of church music is in no small degree the story of human nature, sometimes in its less attractive aspects. Throughout its development secular music has proceeded normally, has generally avoided entangling alliances, and has asked acceptance solely on its merits as music. There are, to be sure, instances where sacred as well as secular music has gained spurious recognition through the literary excellence of its text, a feature which composers could not match with their music; and there have been cases where the eloquence of the music has carried the day even though the literary inferiority of the text was only emphasized thereby. But in general the music of the world has stood squarely on its own feet, relying on a just and sane partnership between text and music, free from dictation, requir-

---

[1] This book is in no sense a history of church music, the occasional introduction of historical material being for the purpose of pointing up some practical issue. The reader is referred to the *History of Church Music* in two volumes by Professor Leo Schrade and Dr. Beekman Cannon, both of Yale University, shortly to be issued by Harper and Brothers of New York City.

ing no exceptional circumstances for its performance, and indulging in no special pleading based in such traits of human nature as prejudice and sectarianism. The course of church music, on the other hand, never has run smoothly. What is good and what is bad has ever been a vexed question. The church's ideal was at first expressed in music as beautiful, as natural, and as logically suited to the fulfillment of that ideal as folksong is suited to convey the aspirations of a whole people. At times in its career sacred music has achieved an eloquence that was Pentecostal; at others it has spoken the commonest language of the music of the world.

A further difference between these two art types lies in the fact that while secular music displays a single thread of purpose throughout, the history of sacred music divides itself, at the beginning of the sixteenth century, into two distinct and individual lines, the Roman Catholic and the Protestant. However much church music may now have become a commonplace and a matter of no concern, it must be said that in the past the Roman Church has often made sincere if ineffective efforts to preserve her musical integrity. The Protestant Church, too, began with a magnificent ideal vested, as was the Roman, in a single type of music; but that ideal was, for the greater part, eventually dissipated by doctrinal differences and by changes in musical style. Advantage has always been strongly with the older church, for she had over a thousand years in which to establish and develop her theory and practice of music before Luther ever gave thought to the musical means most appropriate to the services of the Reformed Church. The fact that the Roman Church was and is a unit under a single authority and discipline renders her capable of insistence on the highest musical standards. In contrast, the Protestant fold is divided in dogma and in church procedure and is quite lacking in any centralized power. While the Roman

Church has been traditionally unfriendly to secular music, Protestantism has been cordially receptive to it. Throughout the Middle Ages almost all music with the exception of folksong and the music of secular groups was the especial care of the Church; it was she who fostered the art in cathedrals, monasteries, and singing schools, surrounding it with rules both numerous and drastic; and if many of the distinctions between the sacred and the secular that she drew now seem to us to have been purely arbitrary, they are, nonetheless, a convincing indication of a sincere belief in the value and importance of her worship music.

From time to time decrees have been aimed at curbing offences against propriety or designed to reëmphasize the significance of the basic musical tenets of the Church. Ecclesiastical councils have debated the musical question and have recalled composers to a sense of their high privilege. In the great era of missionary effort the emissaries of the Church were instructed to replace other systems of plainchant by the accredited chant, the Gregorian. Strict insistence on uniformity of procedure and upon Roman Catholic ideas of what church music should be have more than once assumed such weight as to give them an almost doctrinal significance. Thus the Roman Church by reason of her solicitude for her music, her authority in all matters pertaining to its style and use, and especially by virtue of that incomparable body of music once written for her services should today boast of a single exalted standard. The low estate of Protestant church music is axiomatic, but it is no less than tragic that the older church has to so great an extent forsworn her honorable heritage.

Not a little of the disrepute into which church music has fallen is due to the false autonomy accorded it. The literature of music is divided into a number of artificial categories such as dance music, school music, theater music, community music, and church or ecclesiastical or worship music, and once a piece is described as "church music" it becomes, to the lay mind, sacrosanct; an entity so special in its nature and prerogatives as to constitute it an art separate from music as a whole. Actually, there are, at most, three traditional reasons for describing certain pieces of music as "church music": first, church music is so called if it is performed under sacred auspices; second, if the text to which the music is set bears some reference to God or concerns one or another aspect of religion; third, if the music displays on the cover a title or other indication that the contents are to be regarded as church music. Without such guidance the frequent inappropriateness of the material would possibly raise pointed questions—wherefore the publisher, realizing that the thoughtful listener may ask "Why sacred?" adorns the cover with a lily or a cross, and that, of course, is irrefutable justification.

In spite of the fortuitousness of ascriptions like "church music" and "sacred music," the world still continues to read into them a profound significance. Once a piece is entitled "church music" or is printed with sacred words, it is assumed that the musical idea on which the music is based is sacred in character; that the music thereby becomes set apart from worldly connotations; and any parody or even mild derogation of it is viewed as oblique blasphemy. As a matter of fact, not a little of the music current in our churches originated under secular auspices.[2] Albert

---

[2] The most frequently noted case is that of the melody of the Passion chorale ("O Sacred Head Now Wounded") which, prior to its conversion to Protestant use, was sung to the text of a German song "My Peace of Mind Is Shattered by the Charms of a Tender Maiden." Few worshipers, probably, realize on Good Friday that they are celebrating the death of their Lord in the music of a love song. The melody is a beautiful one, it is a sympathetic reinforcement of the sacred text, and in its original setting it is certainly not widely known. No exception, therefore, may be taken to its use as a hymn.

Schweitzer points out that the Huguenot Church was forced by circumstances to indulge in this practice of borrowing from the store of secular music even more extensively than the Lutheran, but the Calvinists apparently did not entertain a naïve point of view nor cultivate a long-faced air of hushed reverence as our laymen do. "Even Calvin," writes Schweitzer, "had to laugh,—for the only time in his life—when he saw the most frivolous tunes walking along, chastely and devoutly, hand in hand with the lofty poems of David and Solomon."[3] In the absence of any attempt to apply himself to an intelligent consideration of his church music it would at least be heartening to see the worshiper join hands with Calvin and other sensible churchmen, take a comprehensive look at his church music, and have a good, raucous laugh over it.

If it is true, as I believe it to be, that the partition of music into categories such as dance music, church music, school music, and yet others is justified not by anything intrinsic in the music itself, but because these names connect themselves with music through suggestion, association, or the circumstances surrounding performance, or through the employment of music jointly with language in some form, then it may be said that church music is only *music* set off by a manufactured title from the remainder of the art, possessed of no special capacities or limitations, and subject to the same laws and the same analytical processes, both technical and psychological, as all the rest of music. Before undertaking an examination of that segment of music we call church music we should, therefore, answer certain questions relating to music in general: what is music; what is its nature; what is a musical idea; and what does music mean?

---

[3] *J. S. Bach,* English translation in 2 vols. by Ernest Newman (London: A. & C. Black, Ltd., 1923; New York, The Macmillan Co.), I, 20.

I

The Nature of Music
and of Church Music

Music is, above all else, sound; and as an art which exists
in time but not in space, as the representative arts do, it cannot be frozen into immobility. You cannot analyze music
as you would a picture or a statue or a building; you must
apprehend music at the very second of its passing. Upon
this very simple and oft-repeated definition of music as
sound there would be, I am sure, general agreement, but
turning to the next questions—what is a musical idea, and
what does music mean—we discover a marked difference of
opinion. The will to analyze the quality of musical ideas,
to reduce the meanings of music to definition, has been
tenacious. One of the leading questions is whether music
is self-contained, incapable of expressing anything beyond
itself, or whether it can represent ideas which do not, in
reality, belong to it. I am in agreement with those who
hold that music is self-contained, but at the same time I believe that music can represent ideas; ideas, however, which
are uniquely its own. Music therefore assumes the status of
a language, which is based on ideas logically developed and
carried to a conclusion. Would anyone claim that the first
movement of J. S. Bach's Third Brandenburg Concerto is
not based on an idea—albeit a musical idea—logically de-

6

veloped and carried to a conclusion? If, however, one denies to music the status of a language because unlike spoken or written language, and unlike the representative arts, it cannot convey a single, universally understood meaning, then in that opinion I concur. The ideas set forth in a picture of a battle or in a statue of two men wrestling are so self-evident that their meanings are not only plain to every beholder but are also identical in the case of each beholder. Spoken or written language may say "How sweet the moonlight sleeps upon this bank," but music cannot say that. A given piece may generate as many ideas as there are auditors, and a composer even though he attempt to depict a moonlit bank cannot hope to transmit that idea universally through his music even if he labels his piece "Moonlight on a Bank"; for no two persons will imagine the same degree of moonlight or the same bank; and the literal-minded will immediately think of the First National or the Farmers' Exchange.

When a composer writes a piece of music like "Moonlight on a Bank," descriptive music, program music, he expects you to connect with the music you hear the ideas underlying that music. The Overture to *A Midsummer Night's Dream* seems to depict certain characters in the play and to set the atmosphere, because we are told by the title that that is the composer's intention. If we knew nothing of the story, however, the music would be to us only a delightful composition in scherzo style. The music to the "Spinning Song" in Wagner's *Flying Dutchman* sounds to us the very incarnation of the idea of a spinning wheel in motion; but once you remove the text and perform only the music it is not likely that the present generation which knows the spinning wheel only by reputation as an antiquarian device will declare with one voice, "That must be spinning-wheel music." A combination of words and music is a partnership in which each contributes his share to the proj-

ect, but in which neither may assume the functions of
the other. The fact is that words are one thing, music
another; the words, as they are sung, supplying the commonly understood meaning, the music designed to illumi-
nate that meaning in its own way, but incapable of pro-
viding the meaning by itself alone. Music puts forward one
idea—that which resides within itself—and all other ideas
which its sound projects are suggested by the composer in
the form of a text or a title, or are gratuitously contributed
by the hearer himself. The introduction to Beethoven's
pianoforte Sonata Opus 111 is clearly based upon a musical
idea, but you cannot translate that idea into language because the idea was Beethoven's and he added no commentary on the music by which its meaning may be understood. You may, of course, superimpose on it any meaning
you choose, but that meaning is not the real one. In other
instances Beethoven did not hesitate to imply in a title
what he intended the music to convey. The real meaning
of the introduction to Opus 111, then, is *beauty;* beauty
expressed through the self-contained, abstract sounds of
music uncomplicated by any ideas which might be expressed in language; and that, indeed, is the meaning of a
large percentage of great music.

On this matter of the difference in nature between ideas
in the field of art and those conveyed in language, the
aesthetician David Prall has this to say:

It seems unfortunate that when what is expressed in art is called
ideas, it is so commonly thought of as ideas in the sense . . . of
verbal formulation. For the nature of the meaning of such formula-
tions has remained a sort of familiar mystery not to be discussed.
But the whole cast of our training in a system of education through
lectures and books has, in spite of laboratory science and pragmatic
criticism, fed us so exclusively on words, that we can hardly help
being satisfied with the very commonly specious explicitness of language, as if pure verbal content could furnish an acquaintance with
anything but language itself, or for that matter, as if any other sym-

bolism could have meaning and be knowledge without either presenting content other than itself, or referring to events and to the active processes of behavior.[1]

Now although I have covered only a few details which concern the nature of music in the abstract and have spoken briefly of musical ideas and meanings, those details represent, I think, most that is essential to a consideration of the next and primary question: what in view of the known powers and limitations of music in general may we expect from it when it is used in conjunction with religious exercise.

Many of us are deceived by the persuasiveness of the term "church music" to the point of according to the material issued under that designation attributes which the music does not deserve and powers which it does not possess. We are, for example, intent on investing it with the character of a doctrinal protagonist. Never was a more determined effort made to force music to meet this requirement than during the period of the Reformation. Ordinarily we think of differences in religious conviction as limited primarily to dogmatic questions. Details of procedure naturally do become involved; sermon, ritual, creed, or even a specific language like Latin may directly or by suggestion ally themselves to a particular religious body, but these all make their appeal to the intellect first of all, and their meanings are commonly understood. Music is the one language that can play no part in religious controversy because it is incapable of expressing the same idea to numbers of people. As I have pointed out, its text or its title alone may do that. Music, taken by itself, and at its fullest capacity, can never be an apologist for anything save beauty.

Although we would not wish to return to the blood-and-thunder era of church music, it may be worthwhile to

---

[1] *Aesthetic Analysis* (New York: Thomas Y. Crowell Co., 1936), p. 144.

remind those who take their service music lightly that in the sixteenth century it was sometimes literally a life and death matter. Nowhere was this truer than in England where musical style was most intimately connected with religious belief. To be a musician of the Chapel Royal meant that one must not only be prepared to temper his own religious views to the prevailing royal tenet but that he must, as well, under a Romanist ruler write music of a contrapuntal fabric, and serving a Protestant master simplify his technique to suit a more harmonic method. This was not so easy as it sounds for men like Thomas Tallis and Christopher Tye, who were trained in the tradition of counterpoint, a learned and essentially Catholic. tradition. Counterpoint was involved, expert, professional— the music of the sanctuary; harmony was simple, directly expressive, more rhythmical—the music of the people. But Tallis, who wrote a considerable amount of Protestant music, seems to have successfully defied the Biblical pronouncement that it is impossible to serve two masters, for he, in fact, served four, whose doctrines, to say the least, were not uniform—Henry VIII, Edward VI, Mary Tudor, and Elizabeth. It is thought that in spite of outward conformity to Protestant principles Tallis remained, artistically at least, a Catholic at heart, for near the end of his life he selected especially his Latin motets for publication; and wisely, I believe, when we compare these works with his Protestant compositions which, from the point of view of sheer beauty and imaginativeness, are not comparable to his Latin pieces. This artistic inferiority is quite understandable inasmuch as Tallis' Protestant anthems had to embody a more recent and to him less familiar principle in composition (a principle contained in the Protestant method), a perpendicular simplification of the old polyphonic procedure which had been established in the Middle Ages and brought to an amazing degree of efficiency even in the fifteenth century. Not all composers adjusted themselves to the new demands as well as did Tallis. The case of Christopher Tye, for example, is peculiarly interesting. Born about 1497, he lived to see five sovereigns rule over England, and he wrote much music in both styles. His polyphonic works are of rare beauty compared with most of his simpler choral efforts, some of which are strongly inclined toward prosiness. One wonders whether Tye was not himself persuaded that this question of alternating styles was a too vexatious one and that he ought to seek some other outlet for his convictions, for in 1550 he was ordained to the Protestant ministry.

Tye and Tallis were not, however, the only ones who faced the problem of a divided church music style, nor was this the sole source of a composer's troubles. The foremost musicians of the time were well known, and it behooved them to refrain from any appearance whatever of sectarian disloyalty. Merbecke, who set the *Booke of Common Praier Noted*, was arrested for sympathy displayed toward the Reformed Church and barely escaped burning at the stake. Thomas Morley, gayest of the madrigalists, was unwise enough, though a professed Catholic, to correspond with Protestants, and though his accuser said, to quote him exactly, that he discovered "enoughe to have hanged him," Morley's repentance saved his life. Composers of renown were undoubtedly leniently dealt with, but the grounds upon which John Taverner was pardoned, while probably satisfactory to him inasmuch as they gave him his freedom, do nonetheless bear an unpleasant suggestion of that type of special pleading which artists and musicians, according to popular report, are supposed to profit by. Taverner, accused of Protestant sympathies, was never punished; he was, indeed, fully pardoned, the argument which freed him being that "he was but a Musitian." The great William Byrd, perhaps

because of his unique eminence in his own time, was
permitted to remain a loyal Catholic throughout his long
life. Whatever view was taken of the music by the church
of that day, we may be sure that for the composers it was
not adherence to a prescribed style, Catholic or Protestant,
which chiefly concerned them, for that was basically a
technical matter; rather it was a question of those qualities
of beauty in the music which they felt would give their
work enduring life.

Although feeling probably ran as high in Germany
as in England, the approach to an adjustment between
religious belief and musical style was far more practical
and sane in Luther's case. Indeed, the more one studies the
history of church music the stronger regard one has for
the wisdom of Martin Luther. He did not hesitate, in the
interest of the Reformed service, to encourage the composition of music similar to that which had been composed
for the Roman Church. More impressive, even, is the welcome he accorded the music of outstanding Catholic
composers like Josquin des Près and Senfl; and once new
texts had been supplied he was eager to receive the products of Catholic genius into the Protestant musical family.
He was, to be sure, outspoken in his condemnation of the
texts to which this music had originally been set, but the
music, being a separate entity and in no way contaminated
by the surroundings in which it had been performed,
could glorify the Protestant God quite as sincerely as
under its original auspices. Such was Luther's belief. Although he lived at a time when religious controversy was at
white heat, he did not allow himself to be deceived by the
fallacy that music, apart from words, contained any dogmatic implication whatsoever. But Luther's willingness to
welcome to the Protestant service music written in Catholic
style was, in one respect, his undoing. His artistic roots
were firmly fixed in Catholic ground, and perhaps because

he was at war with himself in finding agreement between the finished beauty of the older music and the novel simplicity obviously demanded by Protestant style, he failed to see the consummation of what must have been one of his fondest ideals, that of congregational singing in the fullest sense. It is difficult to determine just how much part the congregation actually took during the earlier stages of the development of the German Protestant service, for the tradition of assigning to the choir the musical right of worship was a strong one. Even when the melody of the chorale had graduated from the tenor to the soprano, which took place after the middle of the sixteenth century, the performance apparently continued to remain in the hands of the choir. In the middle of the seventeenth century Scheidt published a book of chorales with organ accompaniment, and with this the organ began to replace the choir as support to the congregational singing of the chorales; even so, for many years after that time the choir persisted in its share of chorale singing. In fact, we may assume that the eighteenth century was at least half over before the congregational performance of chorales approximated in principle what it is today. For those who are vexed by the remorseless grip which tradition of every sort maintains on the church music of our day, and particularly for those of us who lament the supremacy of the modern choir at the expense of the congregational right to its musical part in the service, it is illuminating and a little comforting, perhaps, to consider what Luther's vision probably was and how long it took to reach fulfillment.[2]

Here, then, are two contrasting attitudes toward the relationship between religious dogma and music. In England, in the sixteenth century, there is obviously a close

---

[2] See Schweitzer, *J. S. Bach*, Vol. I, ch. IV, "The Chorale in the Church Service."

connection between the two; in Germany, on the other hand, the issue is more liberally treated. Luther's precept seems to have been that any music either Roman Catholic or Protestant in its origin was acceptable provided it met the requirements of fitness and of beauty. Luther was right. There is no such thing as Roman Catholic or Protestant music, and failure to recognize that fact has cost our services dearly.

Among the fallacies which beset church music, none is more stubborn in its persistence than that which ascribes to music potentialities of an ethical nature. Music, we are often told, may be either good or bad in a moral sense. This is no fantasy of the modern worshiper; from ancient times to our own day writers have committed themselves with definiteness to this belief. In a sermon preached in 1725 George Lavington declared:

Music is a two-edged sword; capable of quelling the passions, so of giving a mortal wound to vertue and religion; and therefore should always be in sober hand . . . Quick and powerful, and penetrating the minutest parts of the body, and inmost recesses of the spirit, when employed under the banners of religion; but likewise searching, and irritating every evil thought, and intention of the heart, when debauch'd into the service of immorality and profaneness. What ought to kindle a devout affection, may blow up every evil desire into a flame, may be the fuel and incentive of vice.[3]

The error here consists in Lavington's inclusion within an understanding of the word "music" certain details invariably connected with music but not actually a part of it; when the statement is made that music may be good or bad in a moral sense it is not music itself that is meant, but the *effect* of it. It will seem to many like an abstraction to say that music can exist and be truly alive apart from its

---

[3] *The Influence of Church Music; A Sermon preached on September 8, 1725* (Printed for James and John Knapton, at The Crown in St. Paul's Churchyard; and Samuel Mountfort, Bookseller in Worcester: London, 1725), p. 25.

sound. Almost everyone would say, certainly, that until a written page of music is converted into audible terms there is no music; only a lifeless record made up of cryptic characters, incapable of evoking any emotional response. Actually, some musicians obtain a higher degree of satisfaction and a more vivid emotional experience from reading a score than from listening to it. This is true especially of passages and even of whole selections which seem so full of beauty and significance that their fullness may only be realized in an idealized performance more eloquent than any human agency however sensitive and skillful could offer.[4] If, then, it is believed that music possesses the power to work good or ill, it must be admitted that the power resides not only in music *heard*, but also in music *seen*.

The effect of music translated into sound depends in part on the music itself, but also, to a very considerable degree, on the performance. As regards church music, the worshiper, convinced of the innate spirituality which for him characterizes the music of his favorite anthem, would surely find little moral profit in a badly sung or distorted rendition of it. An inordinately rapid performance of the "Hallelujah Chorus," for example, invariably suggests jazz, and the solemn "Crucifixus" in Bach's *B minor Mass*, if taken at a lilting pace and altered in phrasing and other performance details, could be made into something very like a waltz. St. Augustine, speaking of a conviction he was sometimes led to hold, that the banishment of music from the service would constitute a moral safeguard, includes mention of performance as a factor which cannot be disregarded: "Notwithstanding, when I call to mind the tears I shed at the songs of Thy Church, at the outset of

---

[4] The tumultuous choruses in Beethoven's *Missa Solemnis* and the final chorus from Bach's *Passion According to St. Matthew* promptly suggest themselves.

my recovered faith, and how even now I am moved not by the singing but by what is sung, when they are sung with a clear and skilfully modulated voice, I then acknowledge the great utility of this custom."[5] The addition of the parenthetical phrase "when they are sung with a clear and skilfully modulated voice" is an admission that the music alone, without certain required conditions of performance, is not enough to give rise to the pious feelings which Augustine claims. His occasional distrust of music comes from the fact that "the sense does not so attend on reason as to follow her patiently; but having gained admission merely for her sake, it strives even to run on before her, and be her leader."[6] For those who are accustomed to treat their church music as an emotional orgy this passage should give rise to thought, for it mentions reason as a cofactor with sense in the process of listening. Many writers still, like Vida Scudder over sixty years ago, seem either to ignore the intellectual element or, at best, to make little of it: "Music, then, is the ideal expression of emotion; and our question resolves itself into this: Is a purely emotional force, apart from a suggestive cause, or an object to which it may be directed, a desirable or a moral influence?"[7] William James, however, concedes that the intellect may, under certain circumstances, play its part: "Even the excessive indulgence in music, for those who are neither performers themselves nor musically gifted enough to take it in a purely intellectual way, has probably a relaxing effect upon the character."[8] Most persons would,

---

[5] *The Confessions of St. Augustine, Bishop of Hippo,* translated and annotated by J. G. Pilkington (Edinburgh: T. & T. Clark, 1886), pp. 272, 273.

[6] *Ibid.,* p. 272.

[7] Vida D. Scudder, "The Moral Dangers of Musical Devotees," *Andover Review,* January 1887.

[8] *The Principles of Psychology,* 2 vols. (New York: Henry Holt & Co., 1890), I, 125, 126.

I believe, question the value, moral or otherwise, to be gained from an approach to music which was, in James's words, "purely intellectual." An intelligent and productive experience of music represents a simultaneous blend of the emotional and the intellectual. In all this preoccupation with the dominance of feeling in musical experience there is also expressed a persistent doubt that emotional activity achieves any object. Miss Scudder refers to this in the passage quoted, and James, again, warns of the dangers of undirected emotional indulgence:

> One becomes filled with emotions which habitually pass without prompting to any deed, and so the inertly sentimental condition is kept up. The remedy would be, never to suffer one's self to have an emotion at a concert, without expressing it afterward in *some* active way. Let the expression be the least thing in the world—speaking genially to one's aunt, or giving up one's seat in a horse-car, if nothing more heroic offers—but let it not fail to take place.[9]

One might wish that James had been more specific about this concert. The emotions experienced must, like those connected with Sunday's music, depend in part on the nature of the performance. Let us suppose that the listener disliked the music and thought it execrably performed; or that he approved of the program but disapproved of the performance; or that he admired the playing and singing but felt that they were wasted on music of indifferent caliber. Under the emotional urge of any of these conditions would he, then, be prompted to snap at his aunt instead of greeting her genially; or instead of generously relinquishing his seat would he be led to tread with calculated malice on the toes of the person standing in front of him in the streetcar? As for action resulting from the effect of music, I can only say that if it could be proved that a worshiper was impelled to double the amount of his contribution or to help a blind man across the street,

---

* *Ibid.*, I, 126.

it would be a matter for outright wonder; because as far as I know, whatever feeble emotional perturbations are stirred up by church music are likely to eventuate in some such action as attempting to encompass the dismissal of the choirmaster when the music and performance he provides are not pleasing.

Whether or not apprehension over the aimlessness of the emotions generated by music is justified, in certain cases at least music's capacity for inciting to action is well recognized. Soldiers, for example, on entering battle are known to be stimulated by the sound of national or martial music; and one thinks of Klopstock's remark that the "Marseillaise" was responsible for the death of 50,000 Germans, and of the Hungarian gentleman who is reported to have said that whenever he heard the "Rakóczy" he was prompted to seize a weapon and do violence. A milder tribute to the suggestive power of musical sound, quite apart from any composition, was once offered by a churchgoer who declared, in my hearing, that he found the tonal quality of certain organ stops erotically provocative. Where church music is concerned, it would seem unwise to attempt to channel the hearer's emotion in any specific direction. If his music is good church music adequately performed, we should ask no more. I am aware that it is a sorry business for the uninitiated to attempt to interpret the philosopher (and I admit that at a number of points in this chapter I have been guilty of that fault), but I have long felt that an observation made some years ago by Bergson in an informal address (as far as I know never published) exactly represents my own feeling: "Good music," said Bergson, "is good action."

In one respect the quotation from Lavington, offered earlier in this chapter, is significant because it states unequivocally what would seem to be the truth—namely, that whatever influence music may exert on character depends on the moral possessions of the listener. Music may be a reinforcement of good or bad instincts, or of thoughts, some of them perhaps suggested by a text set to music or by music heard at some earlier time. In other words, music is not like human beings, moral and immoral by nature; it consists of symbols which, become sound, may generate ideas that are morally productive in some, and in others ideas which are quite the opposite. Henry Hadow's exemption of music from any moral responsibility is conclusive:

It is the one art in which no human being can raise the false issue of a direct ethical influence. It allows absolutely no scope for the confusion of thought, which, on one side, brought *Madame Bovary* into the law-courts, and, on the other, has taught the British public to regard as a great religious teacher the ingenious gentleman who illustrated the *Contes Drolatiques*. Of course, all contemplation of pure beauty is ennobling, and in this sense music may have the same indirect moral bearing as a flower or a sunset or a Greek statue. But of immediate moral bearing it has none. It means nothing, it teaches nothing, it enforces no rule of life, and prescribes no system of conduct. All attempts to make it descriptive have ended in disaster; all attempts to confine it to mere emotional excitement have ended in degradation. Grant that nations and individuals of imperfect musical experience have not advanced beyond the emotional aspect: that Plato had to prohibit certain modes as intemperate, that governments have had to prohibit certain melodies as dangerous. In almost all such cases it will be found that the music in question is vocal, and that more than half the stimulus is due to its words or its topic. Considered in and by itself, the ultimate aim and purpose of the art is to present the highest attainable degree of pure beauty and sound.[10]

Hadow's mention of "vocal music," "words," and "topic" leads directly to the consideration of another partnership which vies in misconception with that of music and morals; and that is music and words. When you attempt

---

[10] W. H. Hadow, *Studies in Modern Music*, Second Series (New York: Macmillan and Co., 1894), p. 59.

to impress upon the layman that what he reverently regards as worship music is no more than secular music set to sacred prose or poetry, he is likely to ask whether the supremely devotional quality of a text like "Hark, hark, my soul" or "God is love, his mercy brightens" will not so strongly outweigh the effect of any music—even music secular by association—to which those texts might be set, that the result for the listener could be described as truly spiritual. The answer may be found by following the paths taken by music and language respectively, or better, by music and poetry, in conveying their full import to the hearer. The ideas of poetry originate in the intellect and their meanings are generally universally apprehensible. The ideas of music, on the other hand, originate in the imagination and their meanings differ widely in interpretation. When you read or hear read a piece of poetry, that poetry first engages the powers of your intellect, and unless the ideas it expresses "make sense" to you it fails, thereafter, to summon any other of your capacities. If, however, you have comprehended the ideas embodied in the words, the poetry, if the ideas are suggestive and provocative, is then acted upon by your emotions. If you have an active imagination and you are deeply stirred by this particular poem, your imagination may be called into play; if the mere sound of the words is appealing in itself, the euphony of the language striking, this poem will finally make some impact upon your senses. But it is sense first of all that is involved by music, because music is, fundamentally, sound. Unlike the case with poetry, it is not with ideas that you will be immediately concerned but with the sound of the music, and your ears may be busy with that for some time before another sphere of action is reached; but if the sound delights you, your emotional responses will then be called into play, and for many listeners that is the jumping-off point; they enjoy the sound

of the music, it activates their emotions, and after that
nothing takes place. Again, however, the imagination
may make its invaluable contribution to the experience,
and finally the intellect bestirs itself and asks "What is the
true significance of this music? It is delightful to hear, but
it is my part to determine the meaning and the value of
the ideas it sets forth."

So it is that the elements of mind and feeling resident
in us do not come to life in the same order for poetry as
for music. These elements are located at four depths: on
the outside, the senses; behind them the emotions; behind
them the imagination; and most remote of all, the intellect.
Poetry engages the intellect first and the senses last, while
music acts in almost the reverse order. These distinctions
do not in the least concern the layman; for him words and
music are a unit, complete and indivisible. As there is no
recognition of two separate factors, his experience can
include no evaluation of one as separate from the other.
The words of the anthem will have *meaning;* that is, they
will embody a narrative, a precept, or a statement of some
kind conveying an idea which the worshiper understands
and can retell in his own words, but the music, not having
that kind of meaning, will make sense to the worshiper only
if it is in some degree familiar, reminding him vaguely of
music he has previously heard. Attention will focus on
what may really be grasped, namely, the words; and the
music, heard simultaneously, will command only a general
awareness. The result will be that the meaning of the
music will apparently become absorbed in the meaning
of the words. Were the text indecent, profane, or even
mildly inappropriate, the worshiper would react with
proper violence not only to the words but to the music
as well, because the music would seem to him to have a
meaning identical with that of the text. How far apart in
congruity text and its partner music may be, even with

the honest intentions of the composer, is illustrated by
a gospel hymn mentioned in an article of fairly recent
vintage.[11] The author of this article, like other laymen, fails
to identify the text and music of this hymn as separate and
distinct psychological factors in the total experience. "The
workman bowed with toil could lift his head," we read,
"and sing his triumph to the skies. The mother bending in
anguish over her dead child could be comforted by the
sublime faith of, 'Blessed Assurance, Jesus is Mine!'" Now
let us assume that this bereaved mother knows only the
words of the hymn, never having heard the music, and
that some sympathetic friend who is acquainted with both
words and music, but who has no voice for singing, comes
into her presence, sits down at the piano, and simply plays
the silly, wooden-legged, mock minuet that is the music
of "Blessed Assurance." Is it conceivable that any woman
of normal sensibilities would not, in the circumstances,
resent such a callous intrusion on her grief? If there is any
comfort for the sorrowing in "Blessed Assurance" it is
because of the words and in spite of the music. I do not at
all intend to argue that the singing of this gospel hymn
may not do just what the author claims for it—that is,
offer comfort in time of trouble. "Blessed Assurance" may,
indeed, supply an affirmative answer to the question as to
whether a sacred text sung to *any* music might not furnish
a spiritual experience. If that is true, then it is so because
the listener accepts both words and music as an indivisible
unit having but a single meaning.

There remains now but one detail of my question which
has not been considered. Is it possible for a combination
of sacred words and of music that is familiar to us as
secular to result in feeling of a spiritual nature? It seems
to me most important in this case to remember that music

---

[11] Jay William Hudson, "I Feel Like Singing—*Yes indeed!*" *Christian
Register*, June 1949.

strikes first at the outside; at those elements nearest the surface; at our senses, emotions, imagination. It is they that supply the quickest, the most instant reactions. Poetry must begin with the most inaccessible of the elements, the intellect, and then make its devious way outward to our primary responses. Thus, by the time the full import of the sacred nature of the words—particularly if they are unfamiliar—has, through successive stages of apprehension, laid hold of the worshiper, the quick beguiling voice of music has him in its toils. Take, for example, the case of Ethelbert Nevin's familiar song "The Rosary." Here is a piece of music which conforms to the requirements of secular style as they will be set forth in Chapter II; music which so aggressively proclaims its allegiance to the world that almost instinctively we would describe it as secular. To its credit be it said that this composition started life quite openly as the musical conveyance of the text:

> The hours I spent with thee, dear heart
> Are as a string of pearls to me,
> I count them over ev'ry one apart,
> My rosary, my rosary![12]

Yet hosts of worshipers in churches all over the country listen of a Sunday to that melody sung to the words:

> This holy hour, so sweet to me,
> Is fraught with blessings manifold.
> On bended knee I dream and seem to see
> My Saviour's face, His smile behold.[13]

Regardless of whether the worshiper is acquainted with the original text—and it would be difficult to believe that he is not, in view of the widespread popularity so long enjoyed by this song—I venture to think that after eight

_____

[12] This verse from "The Rosary" is used by permission of The Boston Music Company, copyright owners.

[13] This verse from "The Holy Hour" is used by permission of The Boston Music Company, copyright owners.

measures of that seductive melody he will have to get an
almost unimaginable grip on himself if anything like a
spiritual fermentation is going to be set up within him.
This music, you may say, represents an extreme case, and
admittedly it does, but the same disregard of propriety
in varying degree is common in many Protestant churches.

Recalling the church music you may have heard and
scrutinizing it objectively, it will appear that except for
a saving customary sobriety and restraint, much current
church music differs little in style from the milder types
of secular music belonging to the nineteenth century. I
believe that if you were asked to give a stylistic definition
of the Protestant church music of today, you would find
it a difficult matter. It is so routine, uniform, and inevitable
that we rarely trouble to compare it with other styles; we
conceive of it mainly as a practice, as something which
takes place, not as something which *is*. Indeed, when you
consider the various subdivisions of music proper, such
as dance music, you realize that while these acquire their
designations because of their fitness for the purposes to
which they are put, church music is often quite inappropriate to its surroundings. No great degree of perception is necessary to discover in sacred music a mass of
artistic incongruities and psychological ineptitudes. Neither
clergy nor laity is equipped to face what is, after all, a
dilemma arising out of the substance of music itself, and
as musicians we are either not sufficiently idealistic or too
selfish to attack a disorder which ministers to our vanity
as well as to our material support. If this matter is to be
thought through to the end, sincerely and objectively,
then we must look deeper than the artificially imposed
name; we must look behind the lily on the cover, and
even beyond the fact that this music is heard weekly in
our churches, and actually dissect the technical substance
of music with a view to discovering whether or not there

are elements in the musical body which, historically and aesthetically, have proved themselves friendly to sacred style, as distinct from those elements which by tradition and in current practice are native to the music of the world. This, it seems to me, is one road, at least, to the heart of that tangle of illogicalities we call "the music of worship."

II

Technical Differences Between Sacred and Secular Music[1]

The ideal which persisted throughout the best years of Roman Catholic composition was that the music of the service should never be an end in itself; that it should exist to heighten the significance of the great liturgical texts to which it was set, that it should be an ally, selfless, inconspicuous, of the attitudes of worship. Attending Mass, one was not to listen to the music; his attention was to be upon the altar and the meaning of what was taking place there. To that end, all musical effects which called attention to themselves, all that was restless or diverting in the music, these were to be interpreted as unfriendly to the ideal.

Throughout Christian history there has been a free interchange of musical material between the church and the world, but the stylistic differences that finally characterized them were slow in identifying themselves. Even during the fifteenth and the earlier part of the sixteenth

---

[1] In a book like the present one, designed for the general reader, it would seem desirable to deal with musical technicalities only to a degree requisite to an understanding of the thought embodied in the text. A great deal of the material included in this chapter has been set forth in greater detail and reinforced with music illustrations in Part 2 of the author's *Protestant Church Music in America* (Boston: E. C. Schirmer Music Co., 1933).

century the musical language employed for madrigals and Masses was strikingly similar. Allowing for certain refinements which set one apart from the other, a composer undertaking to write a love song was, in general, limited to the musical vocabulary and technical method of church music. Such a near community of expression must have been unsatisfactory, and musical evidence is not wanting that secular music was struggling to free itself from sacred dominance, to establish its own vocabulary and to speak with its own voice. Before the sixteenth century was far advanced the language of music began to expand, and secular music was prompt to take advantage of the resources offered by new technical discoveries. The major mode had always been common to it, melody was becoming more tuneful, and chromaticism, by introducing startling and colorful changes, ministered as no other means could to the emotional implications of the text. Familiar style, really the forerunner of harmony, was a most valuable acquisition. Familiar style was a method by which all the voices, flowing freely in counterpoint, were reduced to a single rhythm, affording a sharp contrast to the customary rhythmic diversity of polyphony. It had been applied by Josquin in the late fifteenth century in his "syllabic" Masses to bring order out of the verbal chaos which beset the church music of his day, and in this it was most successful, for its use resulted in all the performers singing the same word or syllable simultaneously. No less pertinent was it to the needs of secular music, because if you are listening to a setting of a poem about love or shepherdesses the words are quite as necessary to you as are the "Gloria in excelsis" or the "Cum sancto spiritu" under ecclesiastical circumstances.

The progress of secular music was rapid. Unfettered by church dictation, owing little to tradition, it proceeded to take unto itself the new and engaging devices made

possible by an expanding technique. It could march and
dance, it could imitate the calls of birds, the sounds of
battle, or the chatter of ladies in animated conversation.
But chiefly, it could characterize neatly every aspect of
secular love. In short, it brought music close to reality; and
whereas in a previous age it was mainly the texts that
touched upon existence as it befell outside the church, now
both words and music could combine in a joint, vivid
portrayal of secular experience. By the seventeenth century
music was in possession of all the technical elements needed
for the conveyance of secular ideas, and by the eighteenth
century the wheel had made a full turn and again the world
and the church were drawing on a common fund of
speech; but this time the church—the Roman Catholic
part of it, at least—was the debtor.

Most historians, I think, look upon the sixteenth century,
embracing as it does the Protestant Reformation and the
Roman Catholic Counter Reformation schools of music,
as the highest point in the development of ecclesiastical
style, and in recognition of this they refer to the sixteenth
century, especially the last half of it, as the Golden Age
of church music. That period was, equally, the Golden
Age of secular music, including as it did the great English
and Italian madrigalian schools, the French chanson writers,
and the German composers of lieder. The specific differences between the two styles, sacred and secular, may be
reduced to questions of technical detail, and prominent
among these details as they were applied by the two schools
was rhythm.

Rhythm, with is corollaries meter and accent, though
present in almost all the music we hear, is rarely disassociated from other musical elements. It is, incidentally,
the very life of the military march and is an important
factor in works like Chabrier's *España* and Ravel's *Bolero*.
Strongly pulsed rhythm is an incitement to bodily motion

which may, to be sure, take a no more aggravated form than that of foot-tapping or the beating of time with the hand into which Charles II was beguiled by the rhythmically propulsive church music which, out of his background of the French ballet, he cultivated for his own and his court's edification. The Church of the Middle Ages and of the Renaissance, having before it the example of folksong and the dance, and being quite aware of the distracting power of pulsing rhythm as it was represented in these two forms, realized that the presence of a regularly recurring beat would seize upon the attention of the worshiper, if indeed it led him no further astray; and the Church, therefore, carefully avoided rhythm of that kind, making the flow of the music largely dependent on the accent of the Latin text. This principle reaches its highest manifestation in plainsong, the official music of the Roman Church. As should be the case in all vocal music, the text lies at the heart of the whole substance; whatever intimations of rhythm it contains—rhythm, that is, in the form of regularly placed stresses—are the result of the declamation of the text. All the emphasis is laid on the words, on their meaning and their suggestion, and to this end music becomes an utterly self-effacing servant of the text. If this is to be true, then the music must employ no devices of rhythm, such as dotting, which by its impelling restlessness would draw the ear away from its intended object and direct it, wrongly, to the music. Thus plainsong becomes, in reality, a heightened form of speech.

For a long time after unison music had developed into part music, vocal style, at least, made no use of our artificial mathematical subdivision into measures marked off by bar lines. Avoidance of provocative, regular accentual stress was a natural feature of vocal composition. A contributing factor, too, was the composer's assignment at will of any number of "beats" to a single note. The result of this, when spread over the whole body of the music was to produce what we would call a succession of uneven meters, and in modern editions of sixteenth-century music, for example, this feature in its simplest guise is preserved by tying over weak beats to strong ones. It may be said that music such as plainsong, which moves in a flowing line undisturbed by any formal rhythm, is most unobtrusive from a rhythmic point of view. Unless music possesses in a marked degree some quality such as tunefulness or an elaborate chromaticism it is less likely to call attention to itself than is music which employs irregular and diverting devices of rhythm.

Admittedly, there is nothing intrinsic in any rhythm which, per se, places it in either the secular or sacred category. We have only to remember that during a large part of the Middle Ages the triple pulse was used almost exclusively for the music of the Church; but in that period music was as much a science as an art, and, in addition, the predilection for triple meter was partly due to the theological concept of the number three. Triple time was called "tempus perfectum," perfect time; but behind that lay another triple concept, a Beginning, a Middle, and an Ending; Father, Son, and Holy Ghost. While it is obvious, therefore, that triple meter was not foreordained to be the characteristic rhythm of secular music, nonetheless the feeling persists that in our time, in a majority of cases, a basic movement in threes is unsuited to the music of the service. This may only be explained, I think, by ascribing it to the power of association. As I think of the literature of music in general, it seems to me that disregarding for the moment other technical considerations which may affect its nature, behind much of our church music that is cast in threes lurks the seductive shadow of the lilting waltz. Even under the most sacred auspices we are likely to be wafted back into the era of stately dancing; into the far-off happy time when to the moderate measures of the "Blue Danube" a young man selected a partner for the next dance and not, as is now so often the case, an opponent. The whole truth is, of course, that rhythm is but one among a number of ingredients of which a piece of music is made up; and therefore any dictum which maintained that rhythm, influential though it is among the technical components of music, is alone the factor which determines whether or not a piece of music is sacred or secular in character could hardly be maintained.

To regular pulsing, either triple or duple, the Roman Church of the Golden Age preferred for its choral settings the irregular stresses which are characteristic of plainsong; and conscientious composers of our own time have sought to perpetuate that ideal by the use of what might be called "scrambled" rhythms: 6/8, shall we say, followed by measures of 5/4, 3/8, 7/4, and so on. By this method accentual truth in text delivery is assured, and the over-all rhythm becomes fluid, elastic, and basically unpulsed in any regular sense. Rhythm, the one constant in music, and the element most likely to provoke a physical response, even though the urge to motion be repressed as it generally is in church, is not the friend of pious contemplation. The church in earlier times recognized that fact. We have forgotten it.

Melody, while it is by no means so abstract a detail as rhythm, is susceptible of such diversity of treatment as to make it a factor sometimes difficult to confine within a single category. Plainsong is, practically, a melodic abstraction; "Ah, to the Charms of Love Surrender" from Saint-Saëns' *Samson and Delilah* is not a melodic abstraction, it is a melody with a sharply defined personality, as Samson, in the opera, learned to his acute discomfiture. Why, pray, does plainsong seem like the negation of musical personality, always self-effacing, making no claim on its own behalf but bending its will to every inflection of meaning and accent that reside in its partner the text, while "Ah, to the Charms of Love Surrender" fastens on the lapels of your coat and moons at you with such intensity as to make a saint almost regret his vows? (And Samson, be it said, was no saint.) The answer is, in part, that plainsong practically eschews rhythm, while the other is consciously and artfully rhythmed. But the *Samson* piece is what it is by reason of a variety of technical elements among which rhythm is only one; the intervallic structure of the melody is certainly another. Actually, there are two broad classifications of melody: first, melody proper, and second, tunes. A tune is something with which we easily make acquaintance, something which ingratiates itself quickly and which we are likely to find ourselves whistling or humming. The music of folklore is full of tunes, as are the operettas of Sullivan. A melody, on the other hand, does not become one's property so readily. One must know it well before one may understand its full significance. I would define as melodies such pieces as Handel's "Largo," Bach's so-called "Air for the G string," Mozart's "Dalla sua pace," Brahms's "Wie Melodien," and Holst's great theme from "Neptune" in the *Planets*. I would characterize as tunes "Marching Through Georgia," "The End of a Perfect Day," "God Bless America," "Mighty Lak' a Rose," and "Oh, What a Beautiful Morning." Not all melodies, however, not even some of the greatest, would appear to be suitable for inclusion in worship music. Indeed, the more beautiful a melody is from the sensuous point of view, the less desirable it is for the purposes of the church. Melodies of the opulent type have their proper place in the opera house and the concert hall.

It would be wrong to set an invariable order of values with melodies at the top and tunes at the bottom. The most serious defect in church tunes is that they are under-nourished aesthetically and too feeble to be enduring. If the writers of gospel hymns, for example, persuaded that only tunes would serve their purpose, had appropriated folksongs or the music about the "nice young man" from *Patience* or had borrowed others of the deathless and hypnotizing airs from the operettas of Sullivan, the gospel hymn might have become a permanent fixture.

Unsurpassed as representatives of church melody are plainsong and the Reformation chorale. Ecclesiastical music which bases its melodic substance, whether mono-phonic or polyphonic, on these types cannot stray far from the truth. Such melodies might be characterized as "con-trapuntal" melodies in the sense that they conform readily to contrapuntal treatment. In such a union they need lose nothing of their melodic integrity. Indeed, many of the contrapuntal voices of sixteenth-century church music, including inner voices, are marked by great dignity and nobility.

A technical device much used in melody but common to rhythm, harmony, and counterpoint as well is the sequence, a pattern repeated perhaps three times without interruption. The sequence says, in effect, "Acquaintance with my musical personality is so rewarding that I cannot risk your not getting to know me really well. If you don't appreciate me at a first hearing, it is certain that after a second or third presentation of myself you cannot possibly ignore me." Composers of sacred music in the Golden Age were notably reticent in their use of the sequence, while at the same time secular writers were making ample use of it. In much of the church music of our day it oc-cupies a prominent if inappropriate place.

Counterpoint is the writing of simultaneous melodies: in other words, a four-part composition written in counter-point would be one in which each voice or part was an independent melody. Harmony, on the other hand, consists of chords; and a chord consists of a vertically arranged group of notes simultaneously sounded. In counterpoint the voices rarely move in the same rhythm; in harmony all the voices move in a single rhythmic pattern. Whereas harmony is made up of one dominating melody, the soprano, all the voices in a contrapuntal composition are, theoretically at least, of equal importance. It is inevitable that in counterpoint there should be a great deal of rhythmic life, as each participant may move at a speed different from the others and all with assorted types of locomotion. On first thought, therefore, the regular and relatively placid progress of harmony which ignores rhythmic diversity would seem more appropriate to the music of worship than counterpoint with its stimulating variety. Quite the reverse, however, proves to be the case, and for these reasons: counterpoint, because of the changing interest created by the simultaneous progress of a number of self-sufficient melodic lines, each one pursuing its own destiny, each one enjoying an independent rhythmic existence, spreads its interest over so many points and over such comparatively long periods of time that at no given moment does it present any one feature which makes an immediate summons to the listener's attention. Thus the general effect of counterpoint may be said to be impersonal and undramatic; while harmony, partly because of the marked individuality of the soprano, but more especially because of the definiteness and rhythmic incisiveness which harmony possesses, may focus attention instantly on a single detail and is, therefore, essentially personal and dramatic. So counterpoint is an ideal musical conveyance for the expression of the corporate attitudes of emotion such as awe, contemplation, or aspiration, but it is a faulty weapon, in most cases, in the hands of the composer who would express convincingly such profoundly personal feelings as secular love, hate, ambition, jealousy, and pain.[2] Harmony has, without question, its value in the simpler types of church music, but its use needs to be regulated with care and it should be called on only under circumstances in which it is practically and aesthetically indispensable.

Chromaticism is the introduction into music of accidentals, that is, sharps and flats which are foreign to the key in which a piece is written. It corresponds somewhat to the addition of spice in the process of cooking. The methods by which chromaticism is employed and the results obtained are, indeed, varied. There is a vast gulf between the subtle and aristocratic chromaticism of Wagner, for example, and the trite alterations resulting in what is known as barber-shop harmony. On the whole, excessive chromaticism tends to enervation; extended and consistent use of it, even ably presented, as in the Franck symphony, makes one long for the direct and forthright language of the diatonic system. In most of its aspects chromaticism is fundamentally romantic, and in some it is downright sentimental. It tends to weaken the fiber of strong music and to render vapid that which is already inconsequential.

---

[2] To discover the superior appropriateness of harmony over counterpoint in secular situations, especially those somewhat weighted on the dramatic side, one has only to apply the test to such an occasion out of real life as a proposal of marriage. What lady, we wonder, would be impressed with the desirability as a husband of any gentleman who turned up to put forward the crucial issue of his suit accompanied by friends prepared to argue his case in fugal form—all the ardor of his pleading submerged in a verbal texture of bewildering complexity, the hero struggling manfully to make himself heard when it came his turn to announce the little five-note subject to the text "Will you marry me?" If, indeed, you are to have a proposal of marriage cast in terms of music, it must be intoned by one voice only, that of the fond troubadour himself, and if he wishes to enhance the effectiveness of his plea he had better arm himself with a lute or a guitar, either of which may be played from a kneeling position, and either of which will allow him to punctuate tellingly the high lights in his petition by brief, pulsatile strokes of harmony.

Nowadays, chromaticism infests church music to such an extent that in more respects than one it suggests in its behavior the serpent in the Garden of Eden. It slithers insinuatingly over the page and in no time at all completely demoralizes the will of what might have been a reasonably self-respecting piece of music.

A consonance is a complete musical effect. A dissonance represents a musical situation requiring something to conclude it satisfactorily. Or it may be said that a consonance is a positive statement by itself which fully satisfies the ear, while a dissonance is equivocal and unfinished. Dissonances vary from the familiar devices which serve to delay slightly the inevitable consonant outcome to the deliberately sharp, disturbing discords introduced into music either to create contrast to the prevailing euphony or to characterize some word or phrase in the text that invites dissonant treatment. From the psychological standpoint dissonance connotes restlessness, dissatisfaction. It is forever projecting us forward to the moment when, in the music, peace shall be restored. The Roman Catholic Church of the Renaissance was aware of the disturbing quality of dissonance, in the same way that it recognized the capacity for distraction that abides in rhythm. But dissonance would not be gainsaid and church music began to cast its eyes, albeit shyly at first, toward Babylon. The stylistic purity of the Golden Age slowly disappeared, and in its place came a richer, more demonstrative language. The casual listener may not, perhaps, detect the earlier signs of change, but they are present, nonetheless, and they take the form not only of a consciously artistic use of dissonance but also of indulgence in a more elastic melody, in chromatics, and especially in an opulence of texture; and all of these command the ear if not the spirit. In this style is to be found a faint prophecy of what church music was to become in the lush era of the 1900's. Dissonance is a sure vehicle of secular emotion, so only the most sparing and controlled use of it is permissible in the music of the church.

Modes are really scales, and the two with which we are familiar are the major and minor. The medieval world, however, was acquainted with as many as fourteen modes, of which the Church recognized only eight, basing upon them the music of plainsong, the established music of the Roman Communion. The minor mode in its most characteristic form did not then exist, but the major mode, known in medieval times as the Ionian, was in common use in secular music, particularly in folksong. Though many folksongs were cast in the Church modes, the Ionian or major was so much in popular use that the Church dubbed it "modus lascivus" and would permit no use of it in plainsong. The major and minor modes have as their final interval a half tone, whereas the most characteristic of the Church modes close with a whole tone. This difference appears at once if one plays the familiar minor mode with its half-tone ending and then the Dorian mode of the Church system with its whole-tone ending.[3] There is a world of difference between music constructed on a mode ending with a half tone and that which closes with a whole tone. It is a strange, unfamiliar, impersonal atmosphere that is evoked by the latter, and modern composers, desiring to create a sense of unreality, have consistently turned to the whole-tone-ending modes as ideally suited to their needs. Such music stands quite apart from typical secular expression, and its sacerdotal quality, its remoteness from the world, may be ascribed in no small degree to its modality.

If the reader will now turn back to the opening paragraph of this chapter he will find that each prescription of the church is met by one or another of the technical subdivisions of music thereafter described: a rhythm that avoids

---

[3] The Dorian mode may be heard by playing the octave from D to D on the white keys of the pianoforte.

strong pulses; a melody whose physiognomy is neither so characteristic nor so engaging as to make an appeal in its own behalf; counterpoint, which cultivates long-breathed eloquence rather than instant and dramatic effect; a chromaticism which is at all times restricted in amount and lacking in emotionalism; dissonance, used only when it is technically necessary or in the interest of text emphasis; and modality which creates an atmosphere unmistakably ecclesiastical.

That the ideal, so admirably partnered by these types of music, was in the beginning the property of the Roman Church in no way vitiates that ideal for the Protestant Communion. Worship may differ in externals, but its object and its essence are the same for all creeds. Owing to the nature of the Protestant movement and the conditions surrounding the initial stages of its musical policy, the main body of Protestant music took a very different direction from that of the Catholics. That direction, however, was not dictated by doctrinal considerations but by questions of expediency. Luther was never deluded into ascribing to music implications which by its nature it could not contain, and in the same way I am sure that in his heart he must have approved the Catholic ideal for church music, inasmuch as that ideal is not narrowly theological but is basically and broadly *religious*, characteristic of any faith that wishes to make its music something appropriate to the spirit of worship.

The stylistic principles which, in the sixteenth century, set sacred music apart from secular are so intrinsic in musical expression that their validity is subject neither to time nor to circumstance; and it now remains to be seen to what an extent these principles representing the implementation of the church's highest musical ideal are retained in modern church music practice.

III

The Present State of Church Music

The present state of church music is not to be regarded as the product of tendencies peculiar to our own time; its roots were securely planted early in the history of the Church. One has only to read the comments of writers in the Middle Ages to discover how many of the features characteristic of church music as we know it were common practice in that period. Such a sharp line of cleavage between the sacred and the secular as was established in the sixteenth century according to the principles cited in the previous chapter was necessarily slow in making its appearance, and arrived only after successive changes in musical style. The Church's ideal, to be sure, was immutable; it was the music that underwent alteration. Unlike the opera and the symphony, sacred music is not artistically self-dependent, and it would be profitless to treat it as though it were. At every step in its progress church music has been conditioned by the requirements of doctrine, by practical considerations, and by the nature of the service of which it has been a part. Indeed, many of the details which were typical of ecclesiastical music and its performance in medieval times may, in the light of the Church's ideal, be explained only as indicative of the

official attitude toward worship as it was then conducted.
The modern anthem and hymn, no less, although they
represent but two departments of the service, are, in
reality, luminous symbols of public worship as a whole;
so that any treatment of the state of contemporary sacred
music is, in effect, a commentary on the attitudes of clergy,
laity, and musicians toward worship as it is manifested in
the Sunday service; and for the background of that music
as well as of the attitudes which make it what it is we must
again turn backward, and this time to periods even more
remote than the 1500's.

In the fourth century, with Constantine's establishment
of Christianity as the official religion of the Roman Em-
pire, ecclesiastical thought turned toward the ordering
and beautifying of the service, and in this music was important. Plainsong was the form adopted by the Church,
and it still remains the unchallenged example of worship
become music. No other voice so fittingly adorns the
Roman service or so ably illuminates its doctrine. In folksong and the dance, rhythm was essential, but plainsong
was the Church's property, and it abjured every musical
device which was primarily the possession of the world;
devices such as rhythm, chromatics, and the sequence. It
rejected accompaniment of every sort, both vocal and
instrumental, and thus kept itself free of harmonic and
contrapuntal complications, as well as those created by
dissonance. In spite of its simplicity and its scorn of any
sensuous appeal plainsong has never, even in those periods
when church music was inclined to sentimentality, lost its
hold on the worshiper's imagination.

It was inevitable that musicians should, in seeking to
enlarge the resources of their art, cause plainsong to
expand into parts with a variety of intervals. Little by
little rhythmic complexity increased, and this was abetted
by the presence of multiple parts, extensive improvisation,

and the opportunity for the virtuoso performer to have unlimited scope for the demonstration of his prowess. These developments furnished lavish opportunity for the promulgation of musical laws, encouraged exploration into the resources of musical technique, and established a lively basis for the development of new forms. As a step in the evolution of the art of music all this is understandable, but as the art of music was at that time preponderantly church music the step was a longer and a bolder one than ecclesiastical authority could approve. So in the fourteenth century there was issued a papal decree which aimed at restoring church music to relative simplicity. It is debatable whether this decree was for any length of time effective in curbing the practices to which the Church objected; certainly the severity of the language in which it was cast admits no doubt of its firm intentions. Nevertheless, the will to explore and expand the possibilities of musical expression was not to be gainsaid, and in the course of the next two hundred years church music again became ripe for reform. Textual complication and Masses based on secular melodies had become common, with the result that in the third quarter of the sixteenth century during the Council of Trent certain definite precepts governing church music procedure were laid down.

The Roman Church was not alone in its concern with musical matters, for early in this same century the Reformed Communion came to grips with its own particular problems. The Roman tradition had assigned the expert music of the service to the choir, and necessarily so, for the intricacies of counterpoint were certainly not for the congregation. Luther's theory of church music could not embrace the acceptance of the choir as the sole musical ministry, for prayer and praise were not to be vicarious. Whatever music was to be performed by the congregation must be susceptible of being sung by everyone. The task of creating hymn texts was probably not unduly difficult; the Reformation poets were certainly not without models to guide them; but the problem facing the musicians was far more serious, and it was twofold: first, to originate some musical vehicle through which the congregation might express itself, and second, the establishment of a body of choir music comparable in significance with the Mass and the motet of the Roman service. The question naturally to be asked is why plainsong, which must have been well known to Luther's followers, was not adopted as the congregational medium, and the answer is that plainsong lacked the one technical element essential in music to be sung by large groups of amateurs, namely, a type of rhythm which could be easily grasped. Nonetheless, plainsong, adjusted to the needs of Protestant singing, did make its way into the repertoire of congregational song.

It is not surprising that in the beginning, instead of attempting to any great extent the writing of their own congregational melodies as later Reformation composers did, the earlier Protestant musicians should have borrowed from sources already existing in their efforts to furnish music for the accumulating body of hymn poetry. In addition to plainsong, popular song was extensively drawn on, and this was reasonable because here was a stock of familiar music "ready to wear" so to speak. Congregational singing was fundamentally a popular movement and it was only natural to turn for material to music then current and widely sung. That music, however, was secular music, and its adoption had to be sanctified by some sort of technical baptism which would purge it of its more secular qualities. If plainsong according to Catholic usage was not desirable for Protestant singing because of its lack of strong rhythm, then popular song was, for the purposes of the service, altogether too rhythmical. When selecting these melodies Reformation musicians must have realized that association with the original secular text was going to be hard to combat, but they realized, at the same time, that the most effective way of negativing that worldly influence would be to "de-rhythm" the music. Indeed, in most cases the only trace of original sin aggressively present in the music was rhythm, and to the exorcising, or rather to the regularizing, of this feature the early Reformation musicians gave great attention. In the end, all insinuating devices of rhythm were piously washed away, and the once unregenerate melody became transformed into the chorale and took up life anew as the servant of the Protestant congregation. Still unchanged it was and of the earth earthy, insofar as the physiognomy of its melody was concerned, but in its movements as staid and even-paced as holy thought itself.

Once the chorale, like plainsong essentially a unison form, had been adopted as the musical battle cry of the German Reformation, it became the task of composers to expand it into parts in much the same way that Roman Catholic musicians had dealt with plainsong. The first efforts in this direction were stilted and sometimes hardly musical, but by the latter part of the sixteenth century the ingenuity and devotion of composers had solved many of the problems which had balked their predecessors, and there were laid the foundations of a form which after a steady evolution culminated in the chorale preludes of Johann Sebastian Bach.

During this same century the music of the Roman branch was undergoing still further technical changes; changes in no way resulting from the dictation of church authority. Composers were writing with a warmth and an emotional appeal foreign to the rapt and impersonal utterance of Palestrina and his school. There was in the dissonant, chromatic, highly expressive music of Nanini and Vittoria the beauty of sound for its own sake that one finds so

often in the music of the southern races. Its emotionalism
and sensuousness prefigured the personal and dramatic
expression which led to the brilliant polychoric style of the
Gabrielis in Venice and culminated in the opera and
oratorio of the seventeenth century. Plainsong, nonetheless, remained the animating source of this music, and for
composers today as in those times its melodic purity and
austerity have furnished a stimulating basis for composition
in extended forms. Again and again one finds the "Dies
Irae," the "Vexilla Regis," or the "Pange Lingua" woven
into the fabric of modern music. William Byrd once referred to a kind of music that was, as he put it, "framed
to the life of the words," and he might well have meant
the whole vocal product of the Golden Age. The miracle
of plainsong wherein text and music combine in a unity
that is indivisible is here repeated in polyphonic guise in
its ultimate and perfected form. If there is any question
as to the unquenchable vitality of plainsong, let it be
remembered that this fund of gentle melody has been the
uninterrupted spiritual resource of the Roman Communion
and for the musicians within it, and that today it is a valued
adjunct to many a Protestant service.

At the close of the 1600's it was evident that both Roman
Catholic and Protestant composers had, in varying degree, adopted the dramatic style, a feature definitely hos-
tile to the unworldly character of the music of the Golden
Age but assimilable within certain limits by the music of
Protestantism. Surrender to the music of the world is man-
ifest in the church music of the eighteenth century, in
the Masses of Haydn and Mozart, for example, and it only
remained for Liszt, Rossini, and other composers of the
era of romanticism and post-romanticism to make the
capitulation final by emphasizing in sacred composition
the theatricality, sentimentality, and introspective rhetoric
which were the trademarks of those lush times.

Out of the very sketchy historical background which thus far has served as the material of this chapter, one fact stands out; namely, that through a large part of the period considered, artistic and ecclesiastical dissatisfaction with church music and the will to improve it are evident. Most of that dissatisfaction, at least the part of it expressed in words, was largely ineffectual because it embodied the feelings of individuals only; those objectors did not spearhead any large reform movement and they seldom presented any specific suggestions for improvement. Admittedly, many commentators had a just grievance and some stated it unequivocally. Their denunciations, however, boil down to nothing concrete; what remains is often eloquently expressed personal irritation amply garnished with adjectival seasoning. On the Church's side, certainly, all strata of administration from haughty popes to lowly parsons have told us that they did not approve of the church music of their time and have left us just there. In most cases, too, their attacks have been directed not against the basic evil in church music but against those who, superficially considered, were responsible for that music: the musicians engaged in the service of the Church.

Criticism today follows the same pattern as of old, its objects being generally the choir, the choirmaster, and the organist. Perhaps because the choir is the most prominent participant in the music of the service it has always been the first target of attack. Ethelred, Abbot of Rivaulx Abbey in Yorkshire, writing in the early twelfth century, was outspoken in his condemnation of choir performance as he knew it:

To what purpose serves that contraction and inflection of the voyce? This man sings a base, that a small meane, another a treble, a fourth divides and cuts asunder, as it were, certaine middle notes. One while the voyce is strained, anon it is remitted, now it is dashed, and then againe it is inlarged with a lowder sound. Some-

times, which is a shame to speake, it is enforced into a horse's neigh-
ings; sometimes, the masculine vigour being laid aside, it is sharp-
ened into the shrilnesse of a woman's voyce; now and then it is
writhed, and retorted with a certaine artificiall circumvolution.
Sometimes thou may'st see a man with an open mouth, not to sing,
but, as it were, to breathe out his last gaspe, by shutting in his
breath, and by a certaine ridiculous interception of his voyce, as it
were to threaten silence, and now againe to imitate the agonies of a
dying man, or the extasies of such as suffer . . . In the meantime,
the common people standing by, trembling and astonished, admire
the sound of the Organs, the noyse of the Cymbals and Musicall
Instruments, the harmony of the Pipes and Cornets.[1]

Equally outspoken in his irritation is one Aitken, an English cleric, writing some eight hundred years later concerning his impressions of American choirs in the nineteenth
century:

A female contralto voice murmering inarticulate utterances, sustained by an organ accompaniment scarcely more audible than
would have been the tones of a musical snuff-box heard at an equal
distance, made me aware, as I rose from my knees, that something
was happening . . . Soon the organ put on a crescendo, and a soprano voice broke in with equally inarticulate utterances, which
presently culminated in a blood-curdling shriek, a bass and a tenor
by this time assisting in the performance which lasted about five
minutes, and concluded without conveying any single idea to my
mind, except one I found to be in some degree sustained by fact—
that I had been listening to very indifferent opera singers. Then
came the reading of the service, the four distinguished persons in
the west gallery apparently taking no part until the *Venite* was
reached. Here came performance the second, the large congregation
standing meekly while the four actors gayly disported themselves
up and down the diatonic and chromatic scales.[2]

These fulminations are typical, and like others of their

---

[1] *Speculum Charitatis.* The passage quoted, translated by William
Prynne in *Histriomastix* (1633 [1632]), is quoted by Henry Davey,
History of English Music (London: J. Curwen & Sons Ltd., 1895), p. 19.
[2] F. Landon Humphreys, *The Evolution of Church Music* (New York:
Charles Scribner's Sons, 1896), pp. 171-172.

kind they imply a dissatisfaction with more than just the singing. Does the choir exceed its prerogatives? What, indeed, are its prerogatives? I assume that one hundred lay definitions of the choir would probably agree in substance, but the dictionary unexpectedly offers supplementary and suggestive information. "A choir," it says, "is an organized company of singers, especially in church." Disregarding the question as to whether *all* the members of any choir may accurately be described as "singers," my mind went on to the word "organized" and I decided to look it up also. An "organization," the dictionary informs us, is "any vitally or systematically organic whole; an association or society." The words "systematically organized whole" I find provocative. Those words imply integration, a fusion of the separate members, a corporate sense of responsibility, continuity, and a planned existence. I have no wish to labor this definition; I leave it to each choirmaster to ask himself whether his choir is really an integrated unit; whether it possesses a corporate sense of responsibility, continuity, and the enjoyment of a planned existence. In view of the overwhelming importance of the choir I am sure that most choirmasters would agree that organization, in the sense of the dictionary definition, would be most desirable. As the situation now exists, however, choir directors know from painful experience that the choir is a pretty constant abrasive; it often represents only such cohesion as is expressed in loyalty to the parish or to the choirmaster; is easily distracted from attendance at rehearsals by the slightest lure of entertainment, and from service on Sunday by rain or snow, by too much heat or too much cold, by sports of sundry natures, by the radio, and by television. I sometimes wonder why the volunteer choir continues to function at all. Church choristers are, to my way of thinking, an unsung race of heroes and heroines. Superficially viewed, there is not much to command their loyalty. Has anyone ever seen inscribed on a tombstone the fact that this man or this woman conscientiously served his or her God through membership in the parish choir over many years? There is a deal of graveyard literature on the subject of husbands and wives who behaved themselves, and on piety in general; but that John and Mary, side by side, week in and week out, mounted to the choir loft and dutifully labored in the vocal vineyard—that, it would seem, represents no virtue at all. Certainly few will attain the posthumous glory of John Cabecca, precentor to the king of Spain. John Cabecca is buried in the great church at Saragossa, and on his tomb is inscribed the following epitaph:

Here lies John Cabecca, the Precentor to our Lord and King. When he is admitted to the Choir of Angels in Heaven, whose society he will embellish and adorn, and where he will greatly distinguish himself by his singing powers, God shall say to the Angels, "Cease, ye calves, and let me hear John Cabecca, Precentor to our Lord the King of Spain."[3]

My sympathies are, indeed, all with the choir, its singing frequently derided, its private lives mercilessly dissected, and its Protestant status, at least, finally reduced to that of a well-intentioned group of amateurs, vocally articulate in varying degree, who perpetuate a harmless and occasionally a pleasant tradition, namely that of supplying the seasoning for the potpourri we call the "order of worship." It is not that the choir asks for praise; the really conscientious choir seeks neither clerical nor congregational appreciation; it only hopes that God looks with a charitable eye on its humble efforts to serve Him. Commendation is even sometimes resented. I once knew a choirmaster who firmly disapproved of compliments on the singing of his group.

---

[3] *Tyler's Quarterly Historical and Genealogical Magazine*, July 1929, p. 69.

To an admiring worshiper he would say, "It is generous of you to praise us; but it is also most disappointing; if you *consciously* liked our music or our singing of it, then we have fallen far short of our ideal. We worship God through our singing, and as a feature purely incidental to that, we try to create for you not something to evoke your admiration, but merely an appropriate and above all an inconspicuous background for your attitudes of worship." I admire that man's frankness and his idealism. Penetrating one segment of the fog of sentimentality and loose thinking that hang over the whole field of church music he had clarified the function of the choir in the service of worship. Having not the slightest knowledge of abnormal psychology or of the vagaries of the religious mania, I shall not attempt to rationalize the behavior of the church regarding music in certain periods of her history. What I do know, however, is that out of centuries of trying to make music accomplish that which by its very nature is totally impossible for it, out of a concept of worship music that has embraced everything from plainsong to the marimba, out of an attitude that has stretched all the way from indifference to fanaticism, this man's precept is the one illuminating and admirable setting forth that I know of the essential dignity and religious importance of the lowly parish choir.

It is not less than startling to read Albert Schweitzer's description of church music conditions in Germany in the seventeenth century and of the significance accorded to the choir. Schweitzer is speaking of the adoption of a new art form into the service, and he says:

This was possible because it was an epoch of living ideals. In the German towns of that time, large and small, we find ideals such as have animated no other citizen communities since the time of the ancient Greeks. Fatal as it was from the political standpoint that religion had become an affair of states and communes, yet by this very means those ancient conditions were renewed in which the citizen community regarded it as its highest civic duty to look to the artistic form of its own religious service. The service is the concern not of the church but of the town. It is not the consistory that engages the cantor and appoints the singers and the instrumentalists for the church, but the town council and the citizens. The reputation and the credit of the town are involved in having an artistic cultus. When Christoph Bernhard, Schütz's favorite pupil, went to Hamburg in 1663, to be cantor and musical director at the Johanneum, "the leading people of the town," so Mattheson tells us, "went as far as Bergedorf to meet him with six coaches,—a distance of two miles" . . .

The town musicians were chiefly intended to assist in the church music. The educational institutions of the town had also to lend their aid to the art. The Latin schools furnished the choirs . . .

One result of this close connection between the educational system and music was that the level of culture among the musicians of that time was higher than it has been ever since . . . On the other hand, this close connection between art and education resulted in every educated person having some knowledge of music, and those who owed their schooling to it remained true to it, to whatever position of dignity they rose. This general diffusion of artistic culture explains the interest,—quite incomprehensible from the standpoint of the present day,—that was taken in the music of the church. To the Protestant towns of that time the artistic church service was what the theatre was to the Greek community—the centre of art and religion.[4]

Schweitzer's words ought to provoke much thought. There is an inescapable nexus, for example, between his statement that he is writing about an age of "living ideals" and his later remark that the interest taken in the music of the church of that time is "quite incomprehensible from the standpoint of the present day." Indeed, it *is* incomprehensible, partly because we view our church choirs as mere service accessories. One would shudder, to be sure, at a reconstruction which would vest in the Boston City

---

[4] *J. S. Bach,* I, 69, 70, 71.

Council, let us say, the authority to appoint our organists and choirmasters; but on the other hand imagination leaps ecstatically at the vision of six automobiles, corresponding to Bernhard's six coaches from Hamburg, sallying forth to conduct the new choirmaster on his initial Sunday to his post at the First Presbyterian Church. The musician of whom I spoke a moment ago, who resented praise of his singers, was indeed a man of "living ideals," for he saw his choir as a dignified institution and not as an amorphous aggregation of incidental personages to be praised or blamed according to lay fancy.

At the risk of being called "dictionary minded" I am going to return once more to Mr. Webster and his definition of a choir, because this time to his other characterizations he adds one which, it seems to me, strikes very near the truth; for a choir, he says, is "a division of angels." Now I will confess that at first this description appeared to me to be fantastically farfetched, and I doubt not that over the face of any choirmaster who happens to be reading these words a nasty leer is at this moment spreading. Indeed, as I looked back over my long struggles with hoity-toity sopranos, sulky basses, patient, plodding altos, and fragile-tempered tenors, no imaginative resource could conjure up even an apocalyptic intimation of ethereal wings. However, it seemed worth while to seek further, so I riffled back the pages of the dictionary until I came to the word "angel," and there I turned up the following: "Angel—a supernatural messenger of God." And that, I may say, is, from the point of view of the congregation, exactly what the choir is—a company of messengers sent by God to furnish musical entertainment for the ladies and gentlemen in the pews. Webster's definition of an angel reads not a "messenger" but a "supernatural messenger"; and that, indeed, supplies the perfect touch, for supernatural creatures do not eat and therefore they don't have to be paid.

I have long been an ardent advocate of the volunteer choir, but circumstances have led me to change my mind to a great extent. I believe it would do much to dignify and solidify the position of the choir if every member of it were paid *something*, at least, for his efforts. The ministry of the clergy is a spiritual one; the function of the choir is, to my mind, to offer to God a sacrifice—in the Old Testament sense, if you like—a sacrifice of the noblest musical art of the church, presented with a consciousness of the high significance of the sacrificial act. If the ministry of the clergy is a spiritual one, then I would say that the ministry of the choir is one of beauty; and there is no wide gulf between them. You can no more speak of your paid amateur choir as "professional" than you can speak of your minister as a "professional" clergyman. Neither serves primarily for pay. Furthermore, while I believe that the real benefit of choir remuneration would be the establishment of a definite status for the choir in the ecclesiastical economy, I think, too, that it would be good for the laity because it would go a little way, at least, toward dissipating the commonly held conviction that music is so much fun that anyone possessing any useful musical gifts ought to be glad to exercise them just for the joy of it.

Perhaps the inclusion in the annual budget of an item for choir salaries might call the attention of the church to the fact that a musical stomach in the choir loft can be just as empty as a clerical one in the pulpit. If parish and clergy could be brought to see that preaching and music represent two official and coördinating ministries, each devoted in its own way to the glory of God, then the corporate self-respect, the sense of privilege, the conviction of responsibility which choirs *ought* to feel, might reasonably follow, and the choir assume its due place in the estimation of the people and in its own eyes.[5]

A sense of the significance of beauty has generally been present in the Christian attitude toward worship. At times this sense would seem to have been hardly more than a reluctant awareness; and in a period or under a religious philosophy which looked on beauty as something destructive of spiritual values, the aesthetic factor in religious exercise has been ignored. On the whole, however, throughout most of Christian history, man, either for his own selfish satisfaction or because he felt it to be appropriate, has adorned his service with beauty in a variety of forms. For many reasons vocal music has been the most evocative of these and it still is, but it would seem that we ought now to take stock of our resources in order to determine where we stand with respect to the choir of the future. The calculated emphasis on instrumental study and on the band which is a feature of public school music education over a large part of this country is leading to a shift of interest away from singing to more spectacular and in great measure less permanently rewarding musical pursuits, a shift which is bound in days to come to affect the choir adversely.[6]

Instrumental music is undeniably important, but it pre-

---

[5] I am quite aware of the difficulties, impracticalities, and perhaps even the impossibility of adopting any extensive system of paid volunteer choirs. It may be that the disadvantages would far outweigh the advantages. I put forward the idea only as a drastic suggestion in the direction of securing for the choir a more stable position worthy of its importance.

[6] The author does not mean to suggest that singing as a department of the school music program is in danger of abandonment; in some sections of the country, notably in the West and Middle West, choral work is often maintained at an exceptionally high level through programs of superior music which evoke the enthusiasm and respect of students. The real danger lies in the failure of school officials to maintain a proper balance between vocal and instrumental music. Any normal youngster with the applauded example of older children before him is likely to adopt as his ideal of a musical experience the blowing of something or the hitting of something in a band.

supposes a sensitivity which is gained first of all through
singing, supplemented by some form of ear-training. By
no means has every child such musical gifts or coodinative
capacity as will permit even reasonable mastery of an in-
strument. Those that are so fortunate have become the
aristocracy of the school music world. If we are to believe the music educator when he protests that it is his
object to develop musicalness in children, then I can only
say that groups of youngsters in gaudy uniforms led by
barelegged maidens with batons is a very shoddy substitute
for musicalness. In a Sunday paper I find the following:
"Sixty-five bands, resplendent in uniforms of school colors
and led by fast-stepping baton-twirling majorettes, brought
the eleventh annual New England Music Festival to a close
here today in a three-hour parade through the heart of the
business district. Officials estimated that more than 25,000
persons watched the procession."[7] When, you may ask, did
25,000 people ever offer the encouragement of their
presence at a school choral concert? What sedate school-
teacher, leading her singers in a rousing Handelian chorus,
would be willing to challenge competition by donning an
abbreviated skirt and heaving her knees up under her
chin in violent alternation? Every encouragement, it is
true, should be given to boys and girls who are ambitious
to become proficient instrumental performers;[8] but singing, be it said, is the sure foundation of musicalness expressed through any medium, instrumental or vocal, and
it is, as many an aged caroller will testify, a lifelong joy.
To substitute for it more spectacular and immediately
appealing features displays not only a shortsighted educational policy but presents as well, from the point of

[7] *Boston Sunday Herald,* May 21, 1950.
[8] The instruments should, of course, possess a reputable literature. By
common report there is a lamentable dearth of string players in this
country, a state of affairs which may be charged in part at least to the
current enthusiasm for the woodwind and brass instruments of the band.

view of the maintenance of efficient church music standards, a dim outlook for the future.[9] Medical science may
eventually make it possible for the lame man to "leap as an
hart," but in view of this educational preoccupation with
instruments we must wonder whether in this fad-ridden
generation the "tongue of the dumb" isn't going to disap-
point the prophet's expectations for it.

It may be true that there will always be an England,
but without the slightest intention of indulging in fantasy,
let me say that I am not at all sure that there will always
be a choir; for it is not beyond imagination that our present
worship of mechanical perfection and of the efficiency of
electronics may, in the end, result in the abolition of the
choir. In case you feel that this is beyond the bounds of
possibility, let me refer once more to a Sunday paper. I
quote: "The juke box has gone to church. Members of
the First Methodist Church don't have to wait for the choir
on Sundays to hear hymns and choral arrangements. A converted nickel-a-record machine has been installed in the
chapel. It plays, for free, religious music and scriptural
quotations."[10] Here, admittedly, is a solution of many dif-

---

[9] Inasmuch as true education is not for today but for the whole of life,
one cannot help speculating about the prospects of these young instrumentalists who are being so highly exploited. Some of them will become
competent performers and some, perhaps, professionals; but if community choruses are few, community orchestras are still fewer, and community bands are no less than a phenomenon. One wonders what outlet
there will be for the amateur brass player at, let us say, the age of sixty-
five or seventy; of his chances of associating himself with some instrumental organization in his home town. The opportunities are not likely to
be many, and if nature and the dentist have begun to play "he-loves-me-
he-loves-me-not" with those all-important front teeth, the chances of
performing fluently his old part in "Pomp and Circumstance" are going
to be few indeed. It is not cheering to foresee the plight of John Doe,
once the pride of his high-school band, turned seventy, not humming
over his bass part while waiting for the choir to assemble for rehearsal
but seated in his parlor, dandling his lonesome tuba on his knee.

[10] *Boston Sunday Herald*, May 21, 1950.

ficulties. Recordings of church music are fairly numerous, and if they became a replacement for the live performance one may assume that the phonograph companies and the purveyors of records would not fail avidly to answer the call to a financial Roman holiday. But there will be many, certainly, who will have second thoughts about the propriety of serving up canned alleluias for the church services. In the first place, discs, needles, and loud speakers are not a satisfactory substitute for the live art of music. Surely there is nothing more alive in this universe than music. Those who heard Beethoven play knew his music in the very flesh. Such an experience is impossible for us, but in the presence of great interpreters we may still feel to some extent the initial heat of Beethoven's creative power. What too often remains to us is not Beethoven, but what is left of Beethoven after the studio technicians have finished with him and he has been filtered through the scientific processes necessary to make him audible. Not a *revivified* but a *reproduced* Beethoven. Unquestionably the phonograph has its valuable uses, but it is and always will be a machine. Beethoven was a human being, as are his interpreters, and Beethoven transmitted through mechanical devices and embalmed in vinylite is not Beethoven alive. Perhaps those of us whose concern is to impress students with the vitality of great music, with imparting a sense of the spontaneity, the immediateness that reside in musical genius, are most familiar with the difference in response resulting from a recorded performance and one presented in person. A two-piano playing of a movement from a Vivaldi concerto will evoke tremendous enthusiasm, considerable interest in the music, and a host of pertinent questions. Given on the phonograph it is received with a kind of fatalistic acquiescence. That is, I am sure, because the student realizes that what he is hearing is a calculated, perfected rendition, and that save for an increasing scratchiness it will sound exactly the same when he hears it for the twentieth time. Psychologically, this is one of the prime defects, albeit an unavoidable one, in phonograph performance—there is no margin of chance. Hearing a record of the Vitali *Chaconne* you know that the violinist has no opportunity on this particular occasion of playing it better than he ever has before, or with a finer interpretation; the performance, as it emerges from the phonograph, is final and unalterable. The player or singer on the stage takes part in a competition; a competition with himself and with the composer; a competition to surpass himself as an artist and to glorify the composer's intentions as he never has before. In the best sense of the word, musical performance is a sport, and the absence from it of the human variable, as is the case with a recording, makes impossible with each new hearing those elements in the listener's approach which are unqualifiedly essential; and they are freshness, novelty, and the imminence of the unexpected.

If these considerations are germane to music education, they are doubly so to worship, for a hymn or an anthem is a valid contribution to worship only to the degree in which it represents the individual personal expression of those actually present. In spite of the literary beauty of the skillfully written prayer, there is much to be said for the ministerially improvised petition that belongs only to a single occasion. If worship music demands for its complete, sincere conveyance the physical presence of the worshiper with a corresponding impression of the here-and-nowness of the event, then any vicarious offering of prayer or praise purchased at a record shop is unthinkable; but not, alas, impossible in fact.

I have accorded considerable space to the choir and to music education as it affects that body, partly because the choir is the most prominent participant in the music of the service and partly because, being constantly and to a great extent unjustly maligned, it has no effective organized means of self-defense as have the organist and the choirmaster who, with the choir, are favorite objects of complaint.

The organist, if his responsibility does not include the direction of the choir, is charged with selecting and playing the preludes, postludes, and other solos incidental to the service, and to furnishing accompaniments to the vocal music as occasion demands. The choirmaster selects the service music and trains and conducts the choir. Much of the criticism aimed at both organist and choirmaster is concerned with performance and not with what is performed. If the singing is louder, faster, or slower than the congregation finds pleasing there will inevitably be protest, and the upper reaches of musical perception in the pews will doubtless cry out against off-key singing; but on the whole, the choirmaster is on safe ground if he produces an adequate choral result, and the organist is secure provided he does not indulge too frequently in obviously unintentional cacophony. This is not to say that organists and choirmasters are uniformly complaisant toward the mediocrity of the music they select; the truth is that it makes no difference what the level of their taste may be; they are forced, in the end, to serve the pleasure of the congregation. But if a choirmaster's training has been well rounded, his musical taste well established, and his idealism strong enough to cause him to tempt fate, he will reject the inherited literature endlessly passed on from generation to generation, a literature that is safe because its comfortableness is never questioned either by clergy or laity, and with it he will cast out the shallow, showy, sentimental products of the many contemporary composers of popular church music. When the protest over the jettisoning of old favorites threatens too strongly he may insert an artful thumb in the dike of his resistance by assuring

the music committee that such improvements as he con-
templates will not necessarily mean an increase in the annual budget for music. No virtuoso singers will be required; only, perhaps, the present volunteer choir which
is capable of performing music that lays few demands on
the singer beyond reasonable vocal ability and a willingness faithfully to attend rehearsals and services. If our man
is brave he will bring into the service at least some of the
great monuments of sacred musical art; if he is wise he
will do this gradually, mixing the new and the familiar; if
he is lucky he will be able to depend on a receptive attitude; if he is not, then his days in that parish are num-
bered.[11]

A great many organists and choirmasters are, of course,
thorough musicians, but more, certainly, are not. Under
existing conditions only a relatively small number of church
musicians have passed through a course of study which
insures a sound and discriminating taste. Their training, if
they are organists, has usually been given over mainly to
a study of the organ which, like the study of singing,
seems often to result in a musical interest bounded, in the

---

[11] The uniformly distinguished quality of the service music at the
Second Church in Boston, where Mr. Daniel Pinkham has been for
some years the organist and director of a choir of about twenty-five
voices, prompted me to ask Mr. Pinkham about the activities of the
church music committee, the constitution of the choir, and the congregational response to the music program. His reply was: "Actually there has
been no Music Committee as such, so many of the complaints have not
been brought to me directly. As to the choir, it is mixed, a couple of paid
voices in each part and the rest volunteers . . . First, the choirmaster must
not have the slightest doubt of the music. If he is not sold on it emotion-
ally and is not convinced of its musical worth, he should not attempt it.
The conductor must transmit his enthusiasm to the chorus . . . The reaction of the laity is bound to be mixed. There are always those who
want the old, familiar works. To use the popular expression 'Don't close
an old door without opening a new one' seems a reasonable basis when
working with church music. There are some 'popular' church compositions that are just plain bad music and these should not be tolerated."

first instance, only by organ playing, and in the second, by vocal technique. Some theory may have been included in the organist's curriculum and, though this is not usual, instruction in choir training. Schools which teach the practice of church music doubtless offer courses in the history and appreciation of church music also, but before ever that information is supplied, the church musician should possess a full understanding of values in music as a whole.

We are too likely to be prejudiced by extreme cases; by choirmasters and organists—and they are numerous—who have no vision beyond the accepted standard or who view their church work as something destructive of professional self-respect and an activity discreditable to them as musicians; and by the choir that pleads for the dismissal of a choirmaster because he is unwilling to allow the singers to select the anthems and refuses to permit what his choir refers to as "cackling at rehearsals," an indulgence permitted by that choirmaster's predecessor.[12] But if self-control in the face of onslaughts from self-assured ignorance and stupidity is a virtue, then among the possessors of that grace church musicians surely rank high, and to lay at their door all the blame for the low estate of music in the church—an attitude too often characteristic of the past as of the present—to make them the convenient whipping boy for the shortcomings of others, is an injustice and a shame.

Now whatever reproach may be brought against the choir, the organist, and the choirmaster, fault in a major degree rests with quite another triumvirate: the composer, the clergyman, and the layman. The composer has the advantage over clergy and laity in that his studies have presumably brought him into contact with a great many examples of superior church writing which he may study

---

[12] This is not a fictional but an actual case.

analytically and which will serve him as models of style. Furthermore, it should be taken for granted that he will conscientiously criticize his own work, avoiding in it the easy popular cliché, the tear-compelling harmonic progression, the brass band effect, and the catchy devices of the operetta. All this he would do were he writing music to be taken seriously, to be criticized as *music*. But this is *church music* he is composing, and the modern church dotes on poverty of invention and commonness of musical expression; it is difficult to believe that much of the choir music currently produced and widely used has been subjected by its creators to a stricter critical evaluation than that implied in mere salability. Such music may be termed "trade" or "commercial" church music, and its primacy in the American church is rivaled only by the Victorian anthem. The practice and the heritage bequeathed us from across the water has not been undiluted profit. English music of the 1800's, composed for boy choirs, has afflicted our churches like a plague. The Victorian anthem is only the Victorian hymn blown up to elephantine proportions, and Sullivan, I take it, confided to the hymnal and to the choir loft most of the material he found too artistically impoverished to be included in his operettas.

The German chorale is the noblest example of Protestant congregational song, and we must regret profoundly that largely owing to the "uninspired" sources of its texts, this Lutheran music proved unacceptable to the English and Scottish churches. On the grounds of sanctified origin no exception could be taken to the Psalms, so the Psalter, always dignified but sometimes monotonous, angular, and uncompromising in melody, became, rather than the wholly estimable chorale, the ancestor of our American congregational song. Musically unpromising as is a great deal of the Psalter, we could wish, nonetheless, that it had not so generally given way to the Victorian hymn, caught in the pale surge of that belated and attenuated musical romanticism which made its unexceptionable way over the England of Barnby, Dykes, and Stainer; a feeble but an apt partner of religious literature frequently devoted to self-congratulation on an almost automatic salvation.

While we are inclined to blame England for much that is bad in our hymns and anthems, she is but one among a number of causes. It is certainly true that the great bulk of the church music of the Victorians often supplies the needs of churches which turn to music which sings well, is easy to learn, and which may be entirely taken for granted. That music is correct and technically sound, but most of it is utterly barren of imagination or of inspiration. The anthem texts never seem to have generated in the composer any musical ideas especially germane to them. Indeed, it is difficult to conceive how many of these texts could have suggested appropriate music. "Arise and Sit Down, O Jerusalem," "It Is High Time," "How Dreadful Is This Place"—from such arid and factual substance one could hardly squeeze inspiration even with the aid of a hydraulic press.

For those choirmasters and churches who welcome it, there is an impressive amount of sixteenth-century material supplied with English texts; if much of this is beyond the capacity of most choirs there is still an ample literature written in three parts according to a method common in the sixteenth century called composition "for equal voices." This music, generally simple, may by literal transposition be performed by any amateur group comprising first and second soprano, and alto; or alto, tenor, and bass. Not only is this music of the first quality, but it is, as well, highly useful for small choirs or choirs of modest attainments. Not a little of this material has been published, but much more remains in anthologies and in library volumes, awaiting publication with English texts for the use of churches which detect a taint of theological sub-versiveness in the Latin language.[18] It is perhaps hardly worth while to mention the magnificent church music of Lassus, Praetorius, and others, written in two parts, or to speak of the great unison literature. Choirs love harmony and resent any attack on their musical integrity which involves singing the same notes someone else is singing.

If I have emphasized the excellence of the music of the past it is with no thought of implying that writing sacred music is a lost art in our own time. In contemporary England and in the Russia of pre-Soviet days there has been a revival of true church style; a revival which has affected both texts and music and which has resulted, through its reversion not only to the spirit but also to much of the technique of the Golden Age, in the closing of a cycle and in the production of music of profound beauty. The causes of the revival are by no means the same in the two countries. The Eastern Church was for a long time the center of resistance to musical change. Like the Church of Rome, she possessed an official chant which represented the core of her musical practice. Indeed, her preservation of the integrity of that tradition was far more persistent than was the case with the Roman Catholic Church, for harmony was not accepted by the Eastern Communion until the late seventeenth century, and disbelief in instrumental participation has been traditional; but the power and persuasiveness of the toxin of Italian musical ideals are proved by the fact that Russia, which of all nations had been the most musically self-sufficient, finally succumbed. The seeds of reform, however, were sown as early as the end of the eighteenth

---

[18] In this music there is a challenge to the serious choirmaster of explorative mind, and every church possessing such an asset should supply him with a machine for the reproduction of multiple copies of this and other music of the past not commercially available. The music of the sixteenth century, incidentally, is not subject to copyright restriction.

century in the work of Bortnianski, and these eventually flowered into a characteristic fervent eloquence that had long been absent from church music everywhere and that came to a tragic end with the revolution in Russia.

The texts upon which this music is founded are naturally those connected with the liturgy of the Eastern Church. The music, while in certain particulars it remains typically Russian, is notable as a revival of the dignity and impersonality of the older music of mysticism. The element of counterpoint, an unfailing presence in the music of the Golden Age, is here replaced by harmony, but a harmony in which all of the voices are of practically equal significance, so that melody in the tuneful sense, even in the soprano, is never invoked. The harmony is not widely varied and is mainly triadic, chromatics are sparsely employed, and rhythm is never prominent as an artistic means save when, for a moment, it ministers to the corporate delivery of some religious sentiment. Restraint and even monotony are typical of this music, but the monotony is calculated and suggests, as did Palestrina's repetition of a single harmony, complete absorption in worship. Separated by almost four hundred years from its logical artistic ancestor and having at its disposal the wealth of material furnished by the steady development of music throughout the intervening years, Russian church music deliberately turned to the past for much of its vocabulary and method.

The present-day English composer, employing legitimate "sacred" devices, has avoided the incorporation in his music of such attractive and musically stimulating factors as rhythm, for example. Indeed, he has gone far toward destroying regularity of pulse and has reconstructed the "just" word and accent of the sixteenth century by various meters used in close succession, such as 3/4, 4/4, 4/8, and 5/4, a technique described in Chapter II. Furthermore, in much English church music the sense of major and minor modality is avoided and the older modality both actual and implied is present. Although originality and imagination seemed to have forsaken English music in the greater part of the nineteenth century, toward the end of that period there appeared evidences of a growing awareness of the suggestive power of words and of a desire to unite text and music in a really significant partnership. Tentative as those indications sometimes were, they nonetheless constituted a prophecy of achievement that has been fully realized in the works of Gustav Holst and Ralph Vaughan Williams. Of great distinction, too, is the music of Healy Willan, now resident in Canada, who has been particularly successful in summoning an atmosphere of unreality by an appeal to the technical substance of a former day. Far different from this is the music heard in most of our churches; and if the result were no more than the deserved humiliation of the profit-minded composer it would be worth while to subject his work to the same qualitative tests as are applied by professional criticism to music not enjoying the unmerited immunity afforded by association with the church. Sentimentality, theatricalism, and introspective rhetoric have, in general, become obsolete; the world as a whole has lost sympathy with the Grand Guignol, the tearful novel, the architecture that is overornate. In music other than that designed for the church, terseness, reticence, and classical objectivity are standard, but not in church music, which perversely remains constant to the superficialities and extravagances of the nineteenth century.

But who will undertake to deal critically with this music? Who is competent to look analytically and objectively at church music and tell us wherein it is deficient? One thinks first of the aesthetician. Beauty is his profession, and it would be profitable to know how he would evaluate contemporary sacred music according to the canons of beauty. I make no claim to extensive acquaintance with writings on aesthetics, but my impression is that philosophers and psychologists are more at home in the visual arts and in literature, passing rather lightly over music, perhaps because the problems involved require a technical knowledge they do not possess.[14] In any case, I can recall no specific reference to church music in any book on aesthetics that I have read. I should not like to see in this an indication that sacred music is not viewed as possessing great importance; more probable is it that the failure to recognize worship music as a separate and idiomatic field within the whole, worthy of special investigation and individual treatment, results from the assumption that church music is no more than music with a functional title and therefore to be held subject to the same considerations as all other music and treated without limiting qualifications.[15]

Or should we turn to the music critic? Rarely does music criticism, in the newspapers at least, focus its attention on the service of worship. Are we to assume that the critic believes interest in sacred music to be too slight to warrant a public expression of his opinions, or is he persuaded that church music is unworthy of his professional consideration? Curiosity prompted me to ask two eminent critics, Olin Downes, of the *New York Times* and Virgil Thomson, of the *New York Herald Tribune*, why reviews of music heard at Sunday services were so infrequent, and

---

[14] Mention should be made of the following works whose authors are not only aestheticians but competent musicians as well: Carroll C. Pratt, *The Meaning of Music* (New York and London: McGraw-Hill Book Co. Inc., 1931); and Elizabeth Woods, *Music and Meaning* (Cambridge: Harvard University Press, 1932).

[15] Although this is true in principle it is to be hoped that someone with the penetrating mind of a philosopher, the full equipment of a musician, and the resources of a psychological laboratory at his disposal will come to grips with the confusing texture of aesthetic factors which confront the serious student of church music.

whether they believed that the quality of church music would be favorably affected if constructive suggestions for its improvement were offered by music critics. Olin Downes replied:

Newspapers have their hands very full in reporting what occurs in the concert halls and opera houses of the land. There is also a general principle, which however is by no means inviolable, especially on the bigger newspapers, to report the nature of entertainment, on the stage, in the opera houses, concert halls, movies, which the public pays its money to hear. This is not at all a merely commercial question, although no doubt the revenue that the newspapers receive from the advertisement of these activities is an important item in their budgets, as indeed advertising has to do with any newspaper, since without it no newspaper could exist or survive. They do not customarily report events which are free to the public unless the events have a special news value. If an important new opera or new symphony were given without charge, or, as often happens on the Times when so great a conductor as Toscanini gives a program for a radio audience of millions, as well as the few people who gather by invitation to hear him at the studio, that is considered news sufficiently important to be reported and critically reviewed.

That is at least one element in the situation and a very important one. The other is unquestionably, the large relative degree of sameness, uneventfulness, and frequently mediocrity, that does obtain in church music and the performances thereof. The church performance of sacred music, on the average, is likely to be a rather commonplace or repetitive affair, from the purely esthetic standpoint.

I doubt very much whether newspaper comment would have any marked effect on the quality of church music. It would seem that any lasting change would have to come from the church itself; from a conviction that change was really needed.

Virgil Thomson wrote:

Most newspapers do not cover church music for two reasons: 1) There is never a large enough staff for that much church attendance every Sunday, already a heavy concert day. 2) Church music, though often excellent, is not presented to the public as a professional act. It is not presented to the public at all, at least in principle, but to God. And God does not necessarily judge acts of

worship by professional standards, since sincerity in His eyes may
well make up for technical inefficiencies.

In general, only those musical events are considered appropriate
for review that are presented to the public as professional occasions. This criterion eliminates church music along with student
recitals and private presentations. Religious music of exceptional
novelty or distinction is now and then reviewed all the same. I
have covered a musical service from time to time at the church
of St. Mary the Virgin, at St. Patrick's Cathedral, at an extremely
primitive Negro meeting house in New Jersey and at a Jewish
temple in San Francisco, where a service composed by Darius Mil-
haud was performed for the first time. One fall I spent all my Sunday mornings for three months going to church services of every
faith and sect, in order to collect material for a Christmas article
about the religious music of notable quality available in New York
City. Religious music presented to the public under concert conditions is regularly covered, of course. In general, however, it is true
that newspapers are not staffed for covering the music of worship,
also that religious establishments might justifiably object to the
public criticism of something not submitted to the general public
for its patronage.

A choir masters' periodical might successfully criticize church
music, but the operation would require standards of judgment far
more complex and delicate than those commonly employed in the
reviewing of concerts and opera performances. My experience in-
dicates that favorable notice of outstanding musical achievement is
welcomed by religious establishments but that any assumption of
the right to judge their cultural standards unfavorably is resented.
Churches are not, after all, primarily purveyors of culture. Their
obligations to music are about the same, I suppose, as those they
assume toward architecture and toward poetry.

Both Mr. Downes and Mr. Thomson are in agreement—
as would be the large majority of critics, I am sure—that
it is not the function of those outside the church or the
church music profession to undertake a critical survey of
the quality of sacred music, and Mr. Thomson's remark
concerning the church's obligation toward music will recall
to the reader the quotation from Albert Schweitzer, cited
earlier in this chapter, regarding the view taken by the

German Protestant Church of the seventeenth century. Mr. Thomson further suggests that a choirmaster's periodical might successfully take over the role of critic; but the critical requirements which, under those conditions, he assumes will give us pause. Certainly the equipment of the average organist or choirmaster as I know it and as it has been described earlier in this chapter would fall far short of meeting the critical standard Mr. Thomson implies.

With regard to their capacities as critics, at least, no major differentiation need be made between the clergyman and the layman. The minister is, after all, only a glorified layman under the skin, and his musical opinions are usually no more to be trusted than those of his parishioners. "Criticism," indeed, is not the word to apply to the attitude of either clergy or laity toward worship music, because too often the intellectual factor, so necessary in all criticism, is lacking, its place being taken by such mental processes as are set in motion by habit and association. It is even doubtful if memory plays much part. After how many repetitions the worshiper could identify the music of a particular hymn or anthem is a matter for speculation, and identification is a much more elementary process than discrimination. Admittedly, a man may, if he happens to be paying heed, prefer one hymn or anthem over another, and the right of preference is undeniable; but its exercise in this case leads to unfortunate consequences because choice will almost always be dictated by personal preference. The layman will, perhaps, "like" one better than another, and having given his opinion he will not be likely to reverse himself. There is a possibility that if he can be induced to sing or even to listen often enough to a piece of church music, estimable but unfamiliar, he may ultimately be convinced of its desirability —provided always that his beauty threshold is not ab-

normally high and his prejudice against *any* new music
is not too strong. The gradual displacement of a poor
hymn tune by a good one, set to the same text, does
occasionally occur, and unfamiliar anthems of admirable
quality do find their way into the choir repertoire; but
when such changes take place it is because of the coming
together of a perceptive clergy and laity and of a coura-
geous and persistent choirmaster having the tact and skill
to make his ideals articulate.

We can forgive the layman much because his faults
of omission and commission are as much inherited as
acquired, but in one particular we can find no excuse for
him, and that is in the magnification of his untutored
and intuitive musical opinions into what seems to him to
be indisputable truth. May I refer again to the article from
the *Christian Register* which serves as a vivid example of
so much that is written and spoken by the layman when
it occurs to him to expose his opinions on church music.
In spite of the fact that the author of that article insists
that he means what he says, it is difficult not to believe
that his words were intended to be what they really are:
a thoroughly delightful parody of the typical layman
writing about church music. But we are bound, however
reluctantly, to take the author at his word. He tells us
that he likes to sing gospel hymns, and without much
effort to establish a connection between this act and his
religious beliefs he leaves us with the impression that the
whole process is mainly in the nature of a catharsis. He
writes engagingly and humorously about all this, but eventually, like so many laymen, he falls into the error of dogmatism. To his credit be it emphatically said, however,
that at no point does he disclaim a knowledge of music.
How profoundly we wish that the man who says "I know
nothing about music" would just leave it at that; too often
we realize with a shudder that we are teetering on the brink

of the qualifying "but," and with the incidence of that lethal word we prepare ourselves for anything from the smug intimation that to display any sympathetic or intelligent attitude toward the arts is to reveal a corrosive weakness of character, on through the various stages of mistaken assurance to a positive dogmatism based on nothing more than grossly uninformed opinion. Assumed omniscience in matters musical is so common that we accept it as one of the painful phenomena of our society, but the assumption of an omniscience that blandly makes God's decisions for him is a rarer though not an uncommon attitude. Thus the writer's account of a harmless old lady proclaiming herself to be, in the words of the hymn, "a sinful worm," and speculating as to her chances of heaven, contains this statement: "I am sure that she will be found just there, at God's right hand, and that God will be proud to have her there."[16] Not, mark you, "If I were God," but positive assurance that God could not possibly dissent from the author's opinion on the matter.

Anyone who feels competent to do God's thinking for him is not going to be backward in passing judgment on musical values. Ignoring the fact that with few exceptions the music of gospel hymns represents no more than a system of vocal calisthenics designed for the exercise of our emotions, the article declares: "The men who made the music of these popular hymns ought to be immortal." And at that statement we experience no shock whatever. The attribution of immortality to composers of meretricious music is a practice not confined to laymen; it is, apparently, in the blood of the whole human race. At another point the writer says, "Lately I met the accomplished organist of a great church who expressed himself of the opinion that certain of our hymns are senseless and

---

[16] Jay William Hudson, "I Feel Like Singing—*Yes indeed!*" *Christian Register*, June 1949.

even vulgar. . . I am afraid that I cannot agree with my friend. The blood of Jesus, what it means, none but his lovers know." Now the author, who whimsically protests from time to time that he is a logician, should have reminded himself once more of that fact and have made some effort to pull together the threads of his thinking. Granted that multitudes of us find unutterable comfort in the assurance of the redemptive power of the blood of Christ, what, pray, has that to do with the aesthetic content of either the texts or the music of the hymns in question; with their senselessness or their vulgarity? Agreement or disagreement with what the author of this article has to say about gospel hymns is comparatively unimportant. What is important is that as a layman he has taken the trouble to write not about the inadequacies of the church musician, as is the way with the few laymen who become church-music conscious, but about the music itself. That is both significant and encouraging. But in the absence of any material body of expressed opinion we must assume that for most laymen Sunday's music has no greater meaning than that of a more or less agreeable or disagreeable interruption of the service.

Agreeable interruptions are of two kinds: active and passive. Among actively agreeable interruptions are those anthems which by reason of some association rouse the worshiper to placid recognition of the fact that a particularly welcome musical acquaintance is present; at some time a nice tune in it or the way it was sung caught the layman's fancy; repeated hearings have enabled him to recognize this piece and perhaps even call it by name. So, all in all, he would say that it was one of his favorites. A passively agreeable interruption is represented by one of a group of old and accepted musical associates, though not necessarily a favorite, which tells the same threadbare story it has told any number of times before, a narrative

cast in musical words of one syllable, so familiar that only
a tolerant awareness of the telling is required. To anthems
like these the layman clings lovingly and with a loyalty
that is stubborn and almost maternal. Their presence, to
be sure, makes no greater impact than does the ringing
of the church bell or the presence of the pulpit, and their
familiarity is, to borrow an expression of D. W. Prall, no
more than "inattentively felt dulness."[17] Their absence,
however, is quite another matter. The withdrawal from
circulation for any considerable period of "O for the Wings
of a Dove" or "Send Out Thy Light" will arouse the layman to high-keyed protest.

A disagreeable interruption is any anthem which does
not slide comfortably along the well-rutted path of the
worshiper's musical consciousness. Is the technical substance unfamiliar; does it contain a few polysyllabic harmonic words; does it ask something more than a physically
open ear? Then, indeed, it is a disagreeable interruption.
Along with this goes the unpleasant interruption represented by the unfamiliar hymn tune. The appearance of
one of these is greeted by the layman with a silence so
disapproving as to be thunderous in its psychic audibility.
If the text is familiar, however, he may, although he has
never heard the music before, try something of his own
in protest. He shares with the choir its determination to
sing in harmony or not at all, and many a man who would
wince with pain on hearing a piece of music cast in the
polytonal idiom will, on Sunday, in preference to singing
the air, blandly fabricate a roving bass in F sharp while
the rest of the hymn proceeds in E flat.

The wraithlike contribution of the laity to the music
of the service has led to the choir's bearing much more than
its due share of the burden. The heart of Protestant musical practice as wishfully ordained by Martin Luther is

---

[17] *Aesthetic Analysis*, p. 182.

congregational participation, and the sum of this is two or three hymns a service, each hymn supplying the opportunity for a kind of ecclesiastical seventh-inning stretch with sound effects. No more salutary jolt could be given the congregation than to declare a five-year moratorium on choir singing; perhaps by the end of that period the congregation, having been forced to sing and to investigate the thoroughfares of the hymn book metropolis other than the well-worn pavements of Duke St., Federal St., and Regent Square, might acquire a sense of its own vocal powers and insist on its fair share of the singing.

For his indifference to the music of the service the layman should not, perhaps, be too seriously taken to task. He is not, as a rule, trained to the perception of musical values. This does not mean that the exercise of judgment, in his case, requires even the shadow of a professional musical training. It means, simply, that his education and experience have not acquainted him with enough great music to allow him to make any rational distinctions between the true and the false, between music that is artistically and spiritually sound and that which is merely a superficial imitation.

If now it is asked, "How on this basis can a Titian be superior to a Varga girl?" the answer would be something like this: In the first place, any man who cannot appreciate a Varga girl is missing something. But, in the second place, a man who has not developed the discriminations to appreciate a Titian is missing something. The second man, moreover, assuming that he also appreciates a Varga, perceives that a Varga girl is little more than a paper substitute for a real girl who is much more worth appreciating than the pictures of her, whereas there is no substitute for a Titian. There really is more immediate pleasure in a Titian for any man of visually refined discriminations.[18]

---

[18] Stephen C. Pepper, *The Basis of Criticism in the Arts* (Cambridge: Harvard University Press, 1945), p. 52.

Whatever may be said for the "visually refined discriminations" of the average worshiper, it is certain that his aural
discriminations are sadly in arrears; and so the Varga girls
rather than the Titians of the anthem world weekly cast
their enchantment over the pews.

The worshiper is not materially encouraged, furthermore, either by the Protestant Church or its services to
attempt an intelligent appraisal of church music. The
typical order of service certainly does not do much to
encourage thought, as it usually consists of a collection
of comparatively unrelated items strung together without
a thread of unity, with no regard for climax, and with
only slight attention to appropriateness. Although the
printed programs of many churches are headed "Order of
Worship" they suggest a most elementary interpretation
of the word "order." The various items do, to be sure,
follow one another in the announced succession, but there
is likely to be a sorry absence of any persisting motif suggestive of the fact that the congregation has assembled for
the purpose of worship. Prayers, hymns, and responsive
readings may be assumed to have God as their direct
object, while with the other activities of the service God
is only indirectly associated. Offertory, anthem, prelude,
and postlude are primarily practical, relaxing, or enter-
taining according to their function; the focal point of the
service is the sermon, and the purpose of that variable
feature is to give instruction. To whom? Not to God, presumably, although I have heard sermons which contained
some pretty pointed hints in that direction. Estimated
numerically or by any other method of calculation, the
non-liturgical Protestant service is heavily weighted in
man's favor, and God comes off distinctly second best.
Yet we call that service one of worship. Intrinsic in worship
are awe, detachment, exaltation, inner peace, contemplation, reverence, a sense of God's mercy, and, by no means

least, mystery. To all of these the best sacred music gives
eloquent voice. When I am in church I sometimes wonder
just what attributes of God are being reverenced in the
music. You may, yourselves, find that an interesting speculation for next Sunday morning.

One of the weaknesses of Protestantism is its failure to
define the meaning and significance of the words "religion"
and "worship." For many Protestants a "religious" man is
one who in all his worldly affairs conducts himself according to precepts implicit in the religion he professes; precepts
laid down by a higher authority in a book called the Bible;
but the visible sign of his religiousness consists in turning
up pretty regularly for the Sunday service. "Worship" is
just plain going to church. Except for recognition of God
as the church's titular head, the Being from whom all our
blessings flow, a Benign Chaperon eager to overlook our
indiscretions, and our Genial Host of a Sunday, there is
little sense of God as a figure whose totality is not to
be comprehended, supreme and all-powerful and above
all to be reverenced; a God "worthy at all times of
worship and wonder." References to God in terms of
profound veneration in scripture or prayer are apparently
taken as little more than high-flown rhetoric. We prefer
the notion of God as a father in the sense of an idealized
male parent whose business it is to safeguard his family
and, insofar as his wisdom will allow, to keep his children
contented. With that realistic concept as a background
it is easy to view the service of worship as an occasion when
our considerate father will be pleased if we are pleased,
and the step from this to almost complete preoccupation
with our own service preferences is but a short one.

The identification of God's will with ours—and I am
sure that this identification could be expressed in some sort
of syllogistic chain reaction—interprets mystery in terms
of reality and ends in a Sunday service permeated by the

presence of our six-day world. The popular Protestant notion of religion is an unrationalized mixture of ethics, piety, churchgoing, and heaven knows what else; one Sunday a year, it would seem, should be dedicated to clarification. It might be called "Definition Sunday," a day on which would be offered sermons on the meaning of religion and worship, explaining that God and not man is the be-all and end-all of religion; and that worship, including music, is a reverent gesture symbolizing recognition of that fact. On the succeeding Sabbath I would implement that instruction by a day to be known as "Worship-music Sunday." At that time I would limit the spoken word to Invocation, Lord's Prayer, and Benediction; omitting prelude and postlude I would restrict the use of the organ to accompanimental purposes only; congregational singing would consist of one chorale such as "A Mighty Fortress" or "Now Thank We All Our God"; the rest of the service I would give over to choir music calculated to discourage critical attention and to be the principal feature in a program which would force the worshiper's musical ear to remain uninterruptedly on its knees for the space of one hour.

Now in spite of Mr. Downes's entirely logical suggestion that musical reform ought to spring from within the church itself, it is clear that efforts toward improvement are too few and too scattered to be of widespread influence. For reasons which have been set forth earlier in this chapter, none of the critical resources I have named—the aesthetician, the music critic, the church musician, the clergyman, and the layman—is truly available. We have no other recourse, then, but to turn to the musician; but, be it understood, a particular kind of musician. If ever there could be a sufficiently large and influential lay group within the various Protestant denominations, persuaded of the inappropriateness and, to put it quite frankly, the sacrilege of offering in God's house, in services ostensibly conducted in his honor, music which on no grounds may be considered proper in those circumstances—if such a group could bring about the appointment of a commission of musicians to select a list of the finest anthems, services, and hymn tunes, and if at least a majority of Protestant churches would agree not to go outside that list for five years, some measurable benefit might possibly result. Such a commission should, I think, be limited to a few members, none of them primarily connected with church music activities; persons of recognized standing in the profession of music and possessing all the qualifications implied in the word "taste." Taste might be defined as a compound of four factors: first, experience, represented by the hearing and, perhaps, the performing of a great amount of music both good and bad; second, a technical training which includes a study of the formal and substantial elements of great music; third, historical knowledge which may be counted on to supply an understanding of the circumstances surrounding the whole development of music and which necessarily involves a broad acquaintance with music itself; and fourth, a sense of style, which is a blend of experience, technical training, and historical knowledge, rendering one competent to evaluate the quality of musical ideas and to judge the appropriateness of their expression. This hypothetical commission of which I have been speaking should not concern itself with the subject matter of the texts except to be sure that they are good from a literary point of view and friendly to Protestant doctrine in general. It is the music, above all, that should be the focal point of its endeavors. The music chosen should include material for choirs of varying ability and should exclude music written expressly for solo and quartet performance. It is understood, of course, that the pressure of expert opinion would not bring about a permanent improvement;[19] but one might hope that musical consciousness in pulpit and pew might stir lightly in its sleep and perhaps ask a drowsy question or two. But even that slight disturbance of the established order is unlikely in view of the absence of any apparent desire for change or betterment.

Change, however, as has been emphasized in the previous pages, has, almost up to the present, characterized the history of church music. The story of the development of church music is the story of the evolution of musical style in general, touched here by genius, there by showmanship, and elsewhere by dullness. No movement, however much devoted to an end which in itself would seem to justify technical and expressive limitations, could preserve its integrity in the face of the experimental spirit of the musical pioneer. It is a fact, furthermore, that of all the separate departments of music, from opera to the music of the dance hall, church music has been the most consistently and generously absorptive; spongelike, it has proved itself hospitable to every musical device that man has found pleasing and profitable under any and all circumstances. Yet in an age that is ardently reform minded, in which old beliefs and old procedures are toppling like ninepins, while the old order—political, moral, economic, social, and even artistic—is being forcefully challenged, we face the phenomenon of a church music that is utterly static. In other fields the will to change is strongly active, not only in the young with whom the characteristics of restlessness and impatience are usually associated but in those of mature years as well. Conscience and conviction are highly articulate and find their expression in every degree from verbal protest to militant action. There are

---

[19] What, in the author's opinion, would be the only lasting cure for the ills of church music will be dealt with in the last chapter.

institutions, some of them of long standing, which remain inviolate; yet in them are to be found the same elements which in other cases have evoked the wrath of the reformers. By agreement of perceptive observers these institutions are in a sorry state, but nonetheless they remain immutable, not because change would be profitless, not because they possess some quality of untouchableness—for no institution in this day may be so described—but simply because their plight is not of a nature to provoke the reformer's zeal nor of such convincing immediacy as to lead to concerted action. Among these institutions church music is certainly one; and this is the more remarkable because among those who ought to be attentive to it are thousands who will spring to action whenever there arises an issue involving some wrong their convictions tell them needs righting. Members of assorted Young People's Societies, of the Ladies' Aid, of the Men's Bible Class will march in processions and picket by the hour in protest against man's inhumanity to man. On Sunday they will sit in mute indifference to music that is an insult to their God.

Such a statement will seem to many like exaggeration or even fantasy, but a large proportion of those service programs which come under my observation sadly prove its truth. Sincere and occasionally effective efforts have been made in an attempt to inject some beauty into the non-ritualistic service, but music has been little affected by these. The church has deliberately laid up its musical treasures on earth, and investment in the trite, the pretty, the sensational, the sentimental, the exhibitionistic, the cheap, the immediately attractive, and the artistically insignificant has resulted inevitably in bankruptcy. If one wished to erect a statue to musical conformity, with countenance frozen in changeless self-satisfaction, he could do no better than to rear a composite figure of the Protestant churches of America. The literary arena is cluttered with the shattered lance points of wasted argument, humble pleading, bitter invective, and provocative sarcasm; all, alike, have been in the past, as they are now, no more than mosquito stabs on the armor of entrenched smugness. Our churches are literally asylums for the harboring of the great army of the apostles of musical mediocrity. For them there are twenty or thirty third-rate musical formulas, and God whom they pretend to worship and who created the free imaginative capacity of man is told that that is all he need expect. Old Handel was unconsciously prophesying all this when he wrote that dullest of dull choruses in *Jeptha* to the text "Whatever is is right." It may be an impious thought, but one might almost wish that church music would suffer a further and progressive deterioration until an aroused laity, recognizing it for what it really is, would finally be driven to revolt against it. Such an apocalypse is surely not near at hand, but it is pleasant to imagine the spectacle of lines of outraged worshipers parading up and down outside the doors of their church bearing placards inscribed: SING TO THE LORD NOT A NEW BUT A BETTER SONG! STAINER MUST GO! THE MUSIC OF THIS CHURCH UNFAIR TO GOD! The widespread and unquestioning acceptance of a service with music that is so reactionary and so open in its discrimination against the Deity is, in this crusading age, a striking proof that the easy tradition of the *status quo* has fastened an apparently unbreakable hold upon the worshiper.

The present state of church music is one to call forth neither pride nor optimism. Representing an amorphous confusion of styles and practices, resolutely excluded from serious thought, beset by whims of personal preference and subjected to the demands of unreasoned purpose, church music, both as an art and as an accompaniment to worship, has become a self-contradiction. Once so vital, so quick to undergo progressive experiment and change, it no longer responds to those influences which affect the rest of music but has fallen into a sleep from which there is, surely, no prospect of an early awakening. For this condition we are all to blame, laymen, clergy, composers, and all musical servants of the church. In us all is lacking the questioning spirit and the religious idealism which animate that spirit. There is, indeed, a vacuum which might profitably be filled with more musical Christians and more Christian musicians.

IV

Church Music and Reality

Up to the beginning of the sixteenth century all church music tradition was vested in the achievement of the Roman Catholic Church, but with the coming of the Protestant Reformation a great change passed over the face of worship music—a change resulting not from any artistic revolution but from the requirements of a new theology. Priestly mediation being abolished, the worshiper was to be his own spiritual advocate; his communion with God was to be direct; regardless of the language employed for worship vicariously offered, his own prayer and praise were to be expressed not in Latin but in his own tongue. In all this music was, of course, included, the congregational medium being the chorale.

It is not necessary here to detail all the technical differences between the chorale and its Catholic analogue, plainsong, but reference must be made to a most signal distinction between the two; that is, the prevailing uniformity of the note values in the chorale, on the one hand, resulting in evenly pulsed stresses and leading to the eventual use of barring, and on the other, the fluid, pulseless flow of plainsong which defied any attempt to confine it within the straitjacket of the measure. Fundamentally the same difference is to be observed between the polyphonic treatment of these two types as is found in their monophonic forms, namely, the irregular stresses of rhythmically diverse counterpoint in the Catholic motet, and the simpler, more regular pulsing of the choral settings of the Reformation hymn. The determination to make the chorale easy to sing both individually and by groups may well have been the reason for the rhythmic definiteness of the chorale, but one cannot fail to recognize a connection between the employment of rhythm and the philosophy underlying the Reformation itself, for of all the elements of music, rhythm is the most personal, the medium through which the individual most naturally expresses himself.[1]

Music, however, was but a symbol of the recognition of the individual as his own spiritual representative, who, if he possesses the right to worship in his own way, has also the right to determine exactly what shall be signified in that worship. One may wonder what Martin Luther would have thought could he have foreseen the tree of many branches that was to grow from this seed of spiritual liberation. The Roman Catholic proclaims his sole allegiance. The Protestant declares himself to be not a Protestant but a member of some Protestant denomination. Thus he conceives of himself not primarily as a humble member of one great branch of the Christian fellowship but rather, through a narrowed focus of interest, as first of all a Baptist, a Congregationalist, or a Methodist. Regardless of the extent to which this disunity may or may not have contributed to the vitality of Protestantism as a whole, its effect on the service and its music has been most unfortunate, because it has helped to prevent the acceptance of any common tradition of public worship. Freedom of choice in the selection of the material of the service, of

---

[1] The author has no intention of suggesting that the presence or absence of rhythm in church music, whether sung by choir or congregation, conditions either sincerity or intensity of feeling. The point is that participation by the worshiper in music of a rhythmic kind comes as near to self-expression as is possible outside the field of secular music.

its hymns and prayers and the order which the various items shall follow, is the right of all denominations and of each parish within them, but this freedom does not include the right to ignore that obligation which is laid upon all religious bodies to include in their services those basic features without which the very word "worship" becomes meaningless.

There is, for example, no universal tradition among the Protestant denominations for beauty as a reflection of the divine. For any over-all, thought-out concept of beauty as it applies to choir music, in particular, there is substituted the casual preference of the laity, and in this preference is found one oblique avenue of spiritual self-expression. Religious interest, contained within successively narrowing circles—Christian, Protestant, denominational, and parochial —finally and unintentionally comes to rest on the worshiper himself. And of this, the outward and audible sign is his church music, a mirror of his artistic insensitiveness and of his egocentricity. Generally salutary, from the Protestant point of view, as was emphasis on the religious independence of the individual, with its accompanying transfer from the impersonality of plainsong to the personal expressiveness of the chorale, the unhappy truth is that when Luther, with the loftiest intentions, decreed that congregational singing of simple melodies should represent a sort of Protestant musical Declaration of Independence, a symbol of man's right to utter his spiritual convictions through music, he released a Pandora's box full of evils that have plagued us ever since, for with the worshiper's sense of his own spiritual authority has grown the conviction that his opinions on everything connected with religious observance are also authoritative and justify a display of the most wilful individualism.

No element in Protestant philosophy is more familiar than individualism. "The pivot round which the religious life . . . revolves," wrote William James, "is the interest of the individual in his private personal destiny. Religion, in short, is a monumental chapter in the history of human egotism."[2] Certainly the demonstration of that self-interest could not escape the most casual observer of Protestant worship, and in that attitude many contemporary thinkers find cause for deep concern. Dean Willard Sperry declared: "Protestant worship is failing everywhere today because it unconsciously suggests that it is not an end in itself, or a suggestion of that end that is announced in the opening affirmation of the Shorter Catechism. Its reference is to man and not to God. It is a means for self-help rather than for self-expression, thanksgiving, dedication."[3] The specific application of that truth to church music is cogently stated by Canon Winfred Douglas in these words: "The main activities and the music of the average eleven o'clock service are directed manward and not God-ward."[4] Indeed they are; and the satisfaction which the music in particular affords the layman is ample proof of Canon Douglas' statement. Outspoken as the worshiper may be in the matter of the anthem, it is the hymn which for many reasons most quickly arouses his critical faculty. The congregational hymn, indeed, may be said to offer the most direct approach to the effect of individualism on church music.

Few hymnals are issued with the idea of elevating the standard of congregational music, and those who are sensitive to mature and aesthetically valid musical speech recoil from a service of worship which includes hymns which cannot be respected as music. I see no reason to

[2] *The Varieties of Religious Experience* (New York and London: Longmans, Green and Co., 1915), p. 491.
[3] *Reality in Worship* (New York: The Macmillan Co., 1925), pp. 248, 249.
[4] *Church Music in History and Practice* (New York: Charles Scribner's Sons, 1937), p. 5.

doubt the truth of Dr. Van Ogden Vogt's assertion when he says, "There are more people of the present generation who have withdrawn from devotion to the church for its failure in beauty than we imagine."[5] If Luther's ideal of religious liberty as expressed in the chorale had been generally realized by Protestantism, if succeeding generations of worshipers had possessed Luther's sound and inclusive taste, if church music had remained a predominantly sacred art, such a comment as I have just quoted would never have been made.

In the previous chapter, in the course of observations on the present state of church music, I have ventured a number of reasons for its sorry condition; to these I would now add another which represents one of the worst evils which lay individualism has inflicted on church music—namely, insistence on reality. The cult of reality is widespread, not only in our church music but in all other departments of life as well. It seems to me that every time I have had what appeared to me to be a really perceptive or productive idea, someone has promptly told me that it wouldn't work; that it was impractical, visionary. I can only say that the older I grow the more disillusioned I become with the apostles of reality. It is to reality, we are told, to things as they are, that we must give attention. I am fully persuaded that it is not the realist but, rather, the imaginative man who sees things as they really are. The realist perceives only what is directly in front of him—the obvious, the immediately compelling issue; he is content with the evidence of a single dimension. The imaginative man, on the other hand, looks around and behind the self-evident facts, seeing them in their total setting, in all their implications; and in the end I am backing him, and not the realist, to come upon the truth.

When the layman says that his church music must be

---

[5] *Art and Religion* (Boston: Beacon Press, 1948), p. 36.

real, he means that it must not be artificial. Like the service, it must involve nothing in which he cannot conscientiously participate; his worship must be without any make-believe; it must be completely sincere. Take the hymns as an example. It is in the hymn that the layman comes closest to actual participation in worship. For whatever sentiments the text expresses he stands sponsor; the voice which utters them is his. Therefore those sentiments must be intelligible to him; they must conform to what he believes; and they must be expressed in a language that is reasonably natural to him; otherwise his contribution to worship will be characterized by insincerity.

Up to this point we cannot seriously quarrel with the worshiper, but we are bound to have a serious difference of opinion with him when he insists that the music as well as the text shall be real. For if the observations which I made on the nature of music in the first chapter are true, then the layman is asking the impossible. One may achieve reality through the mediums of painting and sculpture; language is precise in meaning, universally understood, our common means of communication. But music is exactly the opposite of reality; it is mystery; we cannot see it or touch it; it enjoys no spatial existence; and with a crowning perversity it comes nearest to being real when it turns its back squarely on reality. In a little book entitled *The Passion for Reality* Doremus Scudder, after describing the forms taken by the quest for reality, expresses the opinion that this passion has its dangers: "To us embodied spirits the things most real too often are the things of sense. . . This material world is a real world, and will be as long as men have bodies. Hence the ease with which we identify reality with material things." And later the author comes to this conclusion:[6] "So the passion for things as they are

---

[6] *The Passion for Reality* (London and Edinburgh: Fleming H. Revell Co., 1910), pp. 18, 19, 21.

cheats us into taking the show for the reality, the clothes for the man, the seen for the unseen." If this is true of the representative arts and of literature, as the author elsewhere implies, it is doubly true of music, whose varied language and equivocal meanings easily suggest a reality that is specious. How, then, may the music which is sung to hymns and anthems assume a reality which actually resides only in the words? What constitutes musical reality for the layman? Familiarity, and familiarity alone. In the field of church music, reality and familiarity are synonymous. If, in the hymn, for example, the worshiper is to express himself naturally and fervently, then the music must be cast in an idiom which is not strange to him. So the hymn-book editors supply him with a dozen or fifteen texts set to the same tune which, except for superficial differences, is like 90 per cent of the other tunes of identical meter, all of them made up of familiar, well-worn harmonic, melodic, chromatic, and rhythmic formulas. If these formulas are familiar, they must be common to secular music, for one does not gain familiarity with music by going to church once a week; familiarity comes from singing the songs of the day; from listening to the radio and the phonograph, and from any other musical experience that befalls between Sunday and Sunday. The average layman, if he sings at all, can sing "Home on the Range," "Swanee River," and "Juanita" with a fair amount of vocal competence. These represent, perhaps, the common denominator of his musical consciousness; he feels at home with them and his performing powers are adequate for their requirements. Therefore he resents being asked to express his religious feelings on Sunday in music that is not as natural or as real to him as the music he sings at other times.

Next Sunday, then, with thousands of other laymen we shall rise and sing "Home on the Range." It will not be called that; it will be, let us say, hymn 148. We shall not recognize our old friend because not enough of him will appear at any one time to make recognition possible, but he will be there in every single technical detail; here a little of his rhythm, there a bit of his melody; suddenly a scrap of his harmony; and we shall know that somewhere we have met this amiable stranger before. Decorously he has altered his gait to suit his environment, but when we have got him safely "amen'd" the more observant of us, sitting in our pews, will be grateful that he had the good taste not to mention that "the skies are not cloudy all day."

Although not applying it to music specifically, William James's definition of reality exactly fits our case. *"Whatever things have intimate and continuous connection with my life,"* he wrote, *"are things of whose reality I cannot doubt.* Whatever things fail to establish this connection are things which are practically no better for me than if they existed not at all."[7] Almost every measure of anthem and hymn represents a cross-section of secular and—by transference—sacred musical experience, and in their familiarity they constitute a comfortable reality which resents interruption. It is necessary only to compare the chorale with the hymn in this particular. Absent from the chorale are all the romantic, appealing devices in which hymns abound. Chorales are not the routine stuff of everyday experience. They are, as Canon Douglas has said of them, full of "the note . . . of God-centred worship."[8] Most hymns in current use are drawn from the tritest resources of musical language—bromidic clichés which are to music what typical newspaper English is to literature, the annihilation of everything that is aesthetically stimulating; music without predilections of any kind; music for which there is even no place among the sophistications of modern popular music, which would exclude it as the outworn backwash

[7] *Principles of Psychology,* II, 298.
[8] *Church Music,* p. 229.

of the worst phases of nineteenth-century romanticism.
Yet to God who gave us music this, apparently, is the
best that we can find to offer in return. It is not for us to
speculate as to His musical preferences or to excuse our
insensibility or our lack of musical knowledge; we are
obligated to present in God's house only that music which,
according to the limitations of human judgment, seems
most like Him in character. And if we are incapable of
doing this by ourselves, we should commit it to the care
of those whose decisions may best be trusted.

It is the obviousness, the self-revealing quality of so many
hymns and anthems, that contribute measurably to their
commonness and emphasize the impression they give of
being "real." Indeed, one of the disheartening features of
this music is its lack of reticence. The texts are, many of
them, excellent from a literary point of view, full of dignity
and reserve; they do abundantly fulfill the requirement
of reality; their sentiments are clear and artfully expressed;
as poetry or prose they ring true. But seldom do we match
them with music of like caliber. In a mistaken effort to
make our music similarly real we fall back on the tritest,
most demonstrative secular language of the art.

Let us take two emotions and see how this applies. We
are often told that the music of the sixteenth century is
so archaic as to be incapable of expressing reality; that its
rhetoric is strange to our ears and destructive of active
emotional response to the meaning of the text. Now grief
is something that we have all experienced, and few nar-
ratives either in or out of the Bible appear so much like
the sublimation of all human woe as the story of David
who went up to his chamber and wept for his son.[9] The

---

[9] No more complete or sensitive partnership between words and music
could be imagined than that achieved by the sixteenth-century English
composer Thomas Tomkins in the music which accompanies this narrative.

incident is so remote, the figure of David such a shadowy
one. Yet the Biblical version seems to us almost unbearably
poignant largely because it tells us so little. But turn these
verses or similar ones over to the modern purveyor of
music who appreciates the fact that our layman wants his
music to be real to him, and the composer will strip from
the story all its reserve; the literary frugality of the nar-
rator will count for nought; David will be brought before
us that we may *see* his tears and *hear* his lamentations;
every sentimental device of technique will be exploited
to make the scene realistic.

Not only grief but its opposite as well, joy, we are told,
can find no convincing portrayal in the older music. This
attitude was both stated and in part answered by Richard
Gore when he said:

It has been objected that this diet of choir music is too restricted,
that it leans too heavily on the products of the remote past. In reply, I simply ask, what do we have in our religious life that does
not stem from the past, and from a far remoter past than the 16th
century? The architecture most used in western churches, the
Gothic, comes from the 12th century; many of our favorite hymns
are translations of Latin poems of the first 10 centuries of our era;
the bulk of our Scriptures, the Old Testament, is well over 3000
years old. People should certainly not object, therefore, to using
motets composed a mere four centuries ago. Just as the dramas of
Shakespeare have outlived the productions of hundreds of dramatists
since his time, so the great works of Lassus, Byrd, Schuetz, and
Bach will outlive the shallow ersatz-church music of a later day.[10]

While it may be true, as philosophers say, that our feelings
are not divisible into types such as sacred and secular, I
venture to suggest that the quality of an emotion, or at
least the circumstances under which one experiences that

---

[10] *Church Music in America*, an address delivered before the Toledo
Chapter, American Guild of Organists, at Washington Congregational
Church, Toledo, Ohio, September 21, 1948; prepared for distribution to
ministers and church musicians by the Committee on Worship, Toledo
Council of Churches.

emotion, conditions the manner of its demonstration. The admonition "Rejoice in the Lord" bears no supplementary admonition as to how we shall give evidence of our joy, but I take it that in occidental practice, at least, there is an implied difference between our behavior in such a case and that which would appear suitable under worldly circumstances. Joy is most commonly expressed by physical movement; we dance, or jump, or shout, and whatever we do is likely to fall into some rhythmic pattern. The joy that we derive from religious experience seems hardly to demand such an outlet, yet much of our contemporary church music which centers on this theme conveys its idea by means of music suggesting principally physical exuberance. I do not mean to say that except in aggravated cases composers write music which, in the words of Pope, would "make the soul dance upon a jig to heaven"; but because of the predominance of harmony and rhythm, those dependable allies of secular music, there is a failure to mark any fundamental difference in the quality of mere mundane high spirits and the quieter intensity that characterizes the joy one experiences in God's mercy, let us say. The composers of the sixteenth century had, in the folksongs and dances of their time, all the material they might have required for the writing of sacred joyful music in terms of secular style, but they had no need of using that music any more than we have need of using the secular music of our day.[11]

Considering how great a part the emotions of grief and joy play in our lives, it is perhaps not surprising that so many of us on Sunday accept almost without question a worldly musical interpretation of those feelings. But of all the ideas which would be inhospitable to realistic musi-

---

[11] "This Sweet and Merry Month of May," by William Byrd, is a joyful piece; so, also, is his anthem "Sing Joyfully Unto God"; but in each the composer conveys a very different type of joy.

cal treatment, surely the first would be that of life after death, with descriptions of Heaven and all that relates to that unknown country. In dealing with such texts, two avenues are open to the composer: he may, if he is a genius, attempt to heighten the beauty and remoteness of the words by music that is literally ethereal and disembodied. That has been achieved, albeit rarely. Or he may treat his text as just another aggregation of words and supply for it music that transforms Heaven into a foreign metropolis where life is identical with our own. And that has been done times without number.[12]

We have been examining the effect of lay individualism on service music, individualism expressed in a demand for music that will satisfy the worshiper's requirement of reality. Religion was, no doubt, very real to the early Protestant church, and music was a mighty reinforcement to that reality. The church music of our day, however, is discouraging in many respects; insofar as reality is concerned, it bears witness chiefly to the imaginative incapacity of the Protestant congregation, and to this incapacity the modern composer dutifully ministers. One has only to place side by side the two compositions mentioned in the last note to discover that their creators do not agree even on a definition of reality. It is clear that one of them is thinking of the listener and the other of the text; that the music of one of these selections would do for almost any text, sacred or secular, while the other is exactly suited to the words to which it is set. Or shall we say that the music of one might conceivably be an instrumental piece quite disassociated from words, while the other has no significance apart from its text; that one is intended to catch the ear and the other to quicken the imagination.

---

[12] As examples of two drastically different methods of adding music to words of comfort, the reader is referred to Johnston's "I Heard a Great Voice" (There Shall Be No More Death) and Byrd's "The Souls of the Righteous."

The fact from which we cannot escape is that most church music is vocal music and as vocal music it takes its sanction primarily from the text. Words, as I have earlier pointed out, express nothing but meanings; they are, in that sense, real. Music, in its higher manifestations expresses nothing but beauty; it is, in that sense, mysterious and unreal. Neither may usurp the functions of the other. Words cannot make Beethoven's Eighth Symphony real; only the music itself can do that. Music cannot make real the text "The Lord is my shepherd; I shall not want," because those words are already real. What music *can* do, however, is to make the plain meanings of words glow with an imaginative incandescence sharper and more evocative than, in their literalness, they could achieve. Indeed, among music's great contributions to worship, if we would but permit it, would be its capacity for illuminating those areas above words in which reason cannot operate and where dwell the imponderable, the mysterious reinforcements of the human spirit. To offer to music such an opportunity the composer must, to be sure, make words the compelling source of music that interprets and illuminates, and the best composers both within and without the church have recognized that obligation. But our insistence that church music shall be real has resulted in the use in Protestant services of a shocking amount of pedestrian, commonplace music which does, indeed, satisfy the requirement of reality, but reality of a physical and not of a spiritual nature.

V

The Music of Humility and of Confidence

Our attitude toward worship music is primarily a selfish one. We have come to think of that music not as a vehicle by which we may make our personal contribution of prayer and praise but rather as an adornment which is too often an excrescence, to be judged solely in terms of the performers' competence and the satisfaction the music and their rendition of it affords us. When I say "satisfaction" I do not mean merely aesthetic satisfaction, I mean spiritual satisfaction as well, for the regular pew-holder looks to the Sunday anthem to drive his spiritual thermometer appreciably upward. The power of music to cleanse the heart is estimated in varying degrees; its influence on the criminal whom it will reform, on the juvenile delinquent whose passion for window-breaking it will quell, on the respectable gentleman in the pew who would not inflict even the slightest abrasion on any one of the ten commandments—on them all and on every grade of unworthiness that separates the worst from the best, music is expected to exert an ethical power. The world has not always subscribed to this view, but the modern layman, if he thinks at all about music, confidently expects it to furnish him with what he vaguely terms "religious feeling." Whether or not there exists such a thing as "religious

feeling" is, at least, debatable; but it would be very difficult to persuade most worshipers that what takes place
within them during the course of some lush and introspective anthem is not exclusively religious in its origin but
belongs, rather, within the total area of feeling, being given
religious direction only by association and by the conditions under which it is experienced.[1]

Let us suggest to the worshiper that the direction his
"feeling" takes is likely to be conditioned by the setting
and by allied circumstances, and let us follow the voyage
on which he will be propelled by the fair wind of music
in the form of the typical inspirational anthem from which
he expects to derive spiritual profit. The physical setting
is propitious; he is in church, and presumably when the
anthem begins the shift from the mood general to the mood
specific will not be accompanied by crosscurrents which
will rock his mental boat. But hardly has he left the main
stream of feeling when we find him drifting, and in the
wrong direction. He does not realize this because his sailing orders were clear: they read, let us say, "O taste and
see how gracious the Lord is" or "O for a closer walk with
God, a calm and heavenly frame," and with these words
ringing in his ears his course cannot be wrong. But it can
be, and it too often is. The heavenly breeze the worshiper
had counted on so firmly has played him false. It is an
offshore wind, full of the sounds and scents of this world,
of its opulence, its expressiveness, its sensuous appeal. Sometimes it becomes personified; it beats directly on him in the
moving quality of a solo voice (probably the tenor), and
when it is all over he will insist that because his sailing
orders contained some reference to God he has experienced
"religious feeling."

Is the *music* of the anthem to which he has been listening
sacred music merely because the words were sacred, the

---

[1] See James, *Varieties of Religious Experience*, p. 27.

composition sung in church, or because some publisher
saw fit to print the words "sacred music" on the cover?
Were his emotions really religious? The truth is that many
of us who subject our motives and our actions to the most
careful scrutiny are as naive as Jack Horner when our
emotions are in question. With the use of only one thumb,
you will remember, that remarkable boy was able to extract
a plum from a piece of pastry, promptly deducing from that
accomplishment that he was a good boy. Now I believe
that like all enduring poetry, this verse lays some imaginative burden on the reader. Thus there is nothing in the
picture to suggest that Jack was not a normal boy, and on
that assumption we may conclude that he lost no time in
consuming his prize. But we are bound to ask ourselves,
was it before or after he ate the plum that he said, "What
a good boy am I?" Did his use of the word "good" not
imply that general sense of physical well-being that immediately succeeds on the consumption of anything as
delicious as that plum doubtless was? If we do not read
it so, then this probably innocent boy appears in a very
bad light; for the rhyme volunteers absolutely no information concerning his moral status, and when he says,
"What a *good* boy am I," we actually become suspicious
of his zeal in ascribing virtue to himself in circumstances
involving no question whatever of right or wrong. We are
told that the pie was his, and we assume that in the absence
of parental restraint he could deal with it as he chose; but
his protestations make us wonder, among other things,
whether the plum really *was* a plum, and in the end we give
up the riddle and fasten on the one indisputable fact regarding this boy: namely that he possessed a thumb of
unimaginable magnetic properties. So as we listen to the
music on Sunday, casting our eyes upward in pious self-
congratulation over the "religious" emotion that wells up
within us, we ought to ask ourselves four questions: first,

just what type of fruit is this; second, is it not perhaps too sweet to be really nourishing; third, what possible ethical significance can it have, what correlation with our "goodness," our "religious feeling"; and fourth, is the satisfaction we experience anything other than the result of the impact made upon us by something agreeable and familiar. Now, these feelings of goodness, of spiritual exaltation, are most common to the "melting moods" of religion. They are particularly germane to those states of mind induced by texts of humility, prayer, and aspiration, and as we approach an examination into the manner in which music struggles to convey these words in realistic fashion, we face the nadir of music as a handmaid of religious exercise.

Every man, no doubt, realizes that he could live a more praiseworthy life, but that many of us really view ourselves as "miserable sinners" in the literal, realistic meaning of those words is open to more than a trifle of doubt. I have not, up to this point, questioned the layman's sincerity. I have agreed with his demand that his service of worship shall be real, that the texts of his hymns shall convey to him concepts with which he is in fullest accord; and I have not even chided him for his insistence on reality in his worship music, mistaken and disastrous as I believe that insistence to be. But when he sings:

> With tears of anguish I lament,
> Here at thy feet, my God,
> My passion, pride, and discontent,
> And vile ingratitude.
>
> Sure there was ne'er a heart so base
> So false as mine has been;
> So faithless to his promises,
> So prone to ev'ry sin.

or

> Lord, it belongs not to my care
> Whether I die or live

we may as well squarely face the fact that he does not mean what he says; and if he tries to brush the incongruity aside by referring to "hyperbole" and "symbolism" you can often silence him very quickly by asking him to be consistent in his attitude and put a cross and candles on the table in front of the pulpit. "Rock of ages, cleft for me," "Holy, Holy, Holy! Lord God Almighty!" "Our God, our help in ages past, our hope for years to come"— these are sentiments which he can sing with sincerity; they are, so to speak, foundation stones which underlie his Credo. The music which he sings to these words, provided it offers no departure from routine musical experience, does not much concern him, for as an individual he is only barely tangent to the dogmatic generalities he is pronouncing, and his intellectual conviction that they are true makes emotional reinforcement through music comparatively unimportant. Even in the case of a text like "Dear Lord and Father of Mankind" the worshiper asks of the accompanying music a reality that is mainly expressed in familiar technical formulas. It is, to be sure, an introspective poem, but only mildly so, because its introspection is inclusive—not "my" but "our" foolish ways; and the layman finds that idea intellectually acceptable, because he has only to look about him to see numbers of people who, he knows, are not what they ought to be, singing the same words that he is singing. But once let him change his nouns and verbs from plural to singular; let him sing "Weary of earth, and laden with *my* sin," and his whole attitude approaches artificiality and spiritual falsity. Here, indeed, music must take up all the slack. In order to invest his pose of humility with even a faint show of verisimilitude, music, which could not in the first place express reality because it is merely stuff of the imagination, must outdo itself in order to save the worshiper from self-scorn. So, as he goes through the mental motions of self-abasement he plunges himself into a tearful tide of augmented harmonies, diminished sevenths, and major modes littered with lowered sixths, and comes up almost persuaded that perhaps there is something in it after all.

As far as one may observe from the Catholic music of the sixteenth century, the difference between "I" and "we" was not particularly significant. Humility, like other religious attitudes, was mainly expressed in the corporate terms of counterpoint. Whether one sang "Adoro te" or "Adoramus te" the musical substance was unchanged. The impression we gain from that music is of complete forgetfulness of self, of whole-hearted concentration on God as the object of devotion; whereas the music of humility in which we dress our supplications and plead our weaknesses is so utterly human in all its implications that one feels it is truly as Canon Douglas stated, "directed manward and not God-ward." The first person singular is impressively absent from most of the literature to which that older music was set. "Ego sum pauper et dolens," while not, perhaps, unique, is certainly a text without numerous parallels; and I have not found in the *Liber Usualis* or the *Vesperale Romanum* a single hymn beginning with that three-letter Latin word which in translated form stalks obtrusively through our Protestant hymn and anthem literature.

In Chapter II I dealt with certain features which led to the gradual establishment of secular style and which appeared as natural consequents of an expanding musical technique—features such as harmony, rhythm, and chromaticism, together with a type of melody not to be confounded with plainsong. In such a style were composed the fascinating madrigals, chansons, frottolas, and villanellas of the sixteenth century. But there were yet wanting two elements which should even more definitely separate the secular from the sacred, and these, opera and the solo voice, were thriving before the seventeenth century was old. Neither, as an active principle, was by any means new; but with the first opera and the first oratorio, both of which appeared in the year 1600, the composer found himself possessed of a musical means for the expression of a single personality, as opposed to the impersonal lyricism of the ayre, and to antecedent dramatic presentations such as madrigal comedies in which a single character was represented by a group of singers.

Of the strictly personal attitudes implied in the Christian character, humility and confidence, with their corollaries, seem to call forth the most aggravated manifestations of the weak, the sentimental, and the debased in music, and while in hymn or chorus their commonness may seem to be somewhat mitigated, when confided to a solo voice or a quartet, their triviality is doubly emphasized. Particularly in the setting of prayers for the solo voice is there danger of bad taste. In the first place, the appeal of the solo voice is, so to speak, person-to-person; and by this is meant that the attention of the congregation is bound to be more closely engaged by the performance of one individual than by that of a choral group; to this may be added the fact that few singers are likely to select a solo, however excellent in musical quality, that gives them small scope to express their vocal personalities. Of the solo prayers of my acquaintance, a painfully large majority are plainly addressed to the listener and not to God.

It occurred to me that it would be of interest to examine over a considerable period the course of the expression of humility through the agency of music. To do this logically one must first find a text which represents the very essence of humility, and one which has been treated by successive generations of composers. Ideal in its conformity to these requirements is the "Kyrie Eleison." The Mass is only exceptionally a feature of Protestant worship, and there has never been a continuing tradition of Mass composition in the music of that church. Therefore it is the "Kyrie" as treated by Catholic composers that affords the most satisfactory review, and five examples will serve us.[2]

First, I have selected the "Kyrie" from the *Missa brevis* of the sixteenth-century composer Palestrina. The implications of that music are obvious. There are none of those technical elements which belong properly to secular writing. The music is scrupulously objective and is, as well, both dignified and beautiful. Second, a "Kyrie" by the seventeenth-century Venetian opera writer Lotti, who, for his authority as a church composer, frequently looked to the past. That tendency is exemplified here in the absence of any dramatic content; it is, however, different from the Palestrina excerpt in two striking particulars: it lays considerable emphasis on artistic interest as manifested particularly in dissonance, and it is predominantly harmonic. Third, the "Kyrie" from Haydn's *Imperial Mass*, the Mass in D (no. 3), which offers a striking contrast to both the previously cited compositions. The choral writing is dramatic, and that quality in the music is supplemented by the orchestra boldly imported from the opera house and concert hall. Added to this is the engrossing and spectacular use of the solo singer's art as displayed in virtuoso passages—all, taken together, representing another step in the combination of sacred words and secular music. The worshiper in whom this "Kyrie" could arouse any consciousness of humility would be, indeed, a spiritual superman. I have taken as the fourth example a "Kyrie" from the *Messe solennelle* of Rossini, who is a conspicuous representative of tunefulness in nineteenth-century Italian music. In melody, harmony, and chromaticism this "Kyrie" is thoroughly romantic, and

---

[2] Excerpts taken from these "Kyries" will be found in the Appendix.

so secular in style that it would serve equally well as a
chorus in one of Rossini's operas. The last excerpt is from
the *Missa solennis* by Liszt, whose musical thought dwelt
ever on the pictorial and the dramatic. The theatrical con-
ception of the music is unmistakable. In the exciting trem-
olos of the strings preceding the entrance of the chorus
one senses the hush that heralds the rising of the curtain.
One or more of those musical elements which were identi-
fied in Chapter II as the intimate, personal, dramatic, and
appealing devices of secular music are present in some form
in the last four of these "Kyries," and in the last three,
especially, the music makes no effort to suggest a convincing attitude of humility; the text is merely a verbal
excuse for the making of music intended to be artistically
effective.

There is one other phase of this matter with which I
should like to deal; it is what might be called the "motif
of repose" in the religious poetry of humility. Here again,
music may be destructive of the ideas set forth in the
text; it may be so domestic, so human, so egocentric that
the transaction becomes, in a sense, a transitive verb with
a subject but no object. That, however, is but one symptom
of a change in balance between the human and the divine
which in many services seems to make God an incident
in the business of worship. During the service of worship
the layman's concern is so often over the welfare of his
own soul that one suspects that God is only a shadowy
background for the thought. There must be many who
believe that if these values could be exactly reversed in
the worshiper's mind, if he would think less about himself
and more about God, he would profit spiritually to a
far greater degree. Our church music, particularly our
music of humility, does little to bring this about; it only
eggs us on to greater self-preoccupation.

All this becomes particularly acute in the case of poems

which speak of evening or of death. Whatever the psychological reason for this may be, the sadness and the romance that invest the idea of finality are quickly projected by texts of this kind. It is questionable, in spite of the plain meaning of the words, whether much of this indulgence has any direction at all; whether a great deal of it is not like the vague nostalgia that attacks the adolescent when the wind stirs the grass at sunset or the lights of a train are seen receding into distance. Before sleep the Christian almost instinctively turns to God, and literature contains many magnificent apostrophes written for these circumstances; but once the composer of popular anthems has unleashed the full arsenal of familiar technical devices—then, indeed, thought and spirit will find themselves chained to self and its concerns.[3]

In the previous chapter I compared the old and new musical methods of describing Heaven and the life after death. I want now to revert once more to that idea, but this time from a different point of view, for the motif of repose in its final implications touches man more deeply than any mere objective description of Heaven. Religious poetry, particularly hymn poetry, contains hundreds of morbid and unreal phrases on this subject. How inadequate is the modern church music of reality in this connection I hardly need to point out; the saccharine hymn tunes, the tear-wrenching "we shall miss him" selections of the male quartet, all make of death a purely mundane incident. Here it should be the function of both text and music, by those technical means of which each is possessed, to point out the sole reliance upon which in death the Christian depends, and that though he may in humility confess his

---

[3] If the reader wishes to acquaint himself with two vivid and sharply contrasted examples of the composer's approach to the motif of repose, he is advised to examine Kastalsky's setting of "O Gladsome Light" and the anthem "Sun of My Soul" by Opie.

unworthiness, the final concern is God's and not his own. There exists no finer realization of this ideal, both in text and in musical setting, than the burial anthem composed by Henry Purcell for the funeral of Queen Mary in 1695 and sung on that occasion in Westminster Abbey: "Thou knowest, Lord, the secrets of our hearts; shut not thy merciful ears unto our prayers; but spare us, Lord most holy, O God most mighty, O holy and most merciful Saviour, thou most worthy Judge eternal, suffer us not, at our last hour, for any pains of death, to fall from thee." Here is never music for its own sake but always for the sake of the text; in the words as in the music the two factors in worship, God and man, are present in due proportion one to the other.

It is the quality of emotional antecedent and consequent, so inevitable in the best church music, that was later lost, and with the disappearance of that balance the music became, as in the case of the music of humility, hopelessly one-sided. Fundamentally, the moods commonly associated with worship are not ends in themselves. One does not cultivate the attitudes of adoration, praise, or humility merely to satisfy an ideal of the Christian character; those attitudes, by their nature, must be directed toward some object. The inevitable sequitur of the "Kyrie Eleison" is the "Credo in Unum Deum," and it makes no difference whether the language be Latin or English, the church Roman Catholic or Protestant, those reciprocal attitudes are the same under all circumstances.

Several times in these pages I have taken the product of Roman Catholic composers of the sixteenth century as a point of departure because that music raises no question of a distinction between sacred and secular styles, the substance of the music being fundamentally the outgrowth of a long practice successively pursued by men who were chiefly Church composers writing before the incursion of worldly elements into the Mass and the motet. It may appear to the reader, indeed, that this music of the Roman Catholic Church has been rather aggressively held up as a model. If this is so, it is only because of a conscientious attempt to deal objectively with the matter; for that particular music, it would seem, fulfills two all-important requisites of true church music: first, in vying with the greatest music in any field, sacred, secular, or instrumental; and second, in creating an atmosphere of worship wherein not man but God appears as the important figure in the transaction. This is by no means to say that the Protestant Church does not possess a noble musical tradition, for on the basis of the requirements just set forth, the work of some sixteenth- and seventeenth-century Protestant composers is to be sincerely revered. The fact that the Reformation chorale shares with plainsong the estimation of musicians, that it has often served as the basis of extended composition, and that as a congregational hymn it stands above all others—these are sufficient guarantees of its artistic worth. Furthermore, it is primarily the property of the church, as must be evident when it is compared with the current secularized hymn tune. Any further comparison on aesthetic grounds or from the standpoint of the churchliness of the music of the two faiths must be related to specific composers, for in the field of part music the post-Lutheran anthem was never a serious rival to the Catholic motet. Whether this is to be ascribed to the oft-mentioned hesitancy of the Protestant Church to place much reliance on beauty as an adjunct to worship, or to the superior genius of Catholic composers, or to the rising tide of musical secularism which penetrated into Protestant music almost before it had been firmly established, it is in any case true that prior to J. S. Bach in the eighteenth century there were, excepting Schütz, relatively few highly distinguished composers of Protestant music.

You may classify Bach as a Protestant composer and Palestrina as a Roman Catholic one, but the moods, the attitudes they typify in their music, are universal; those are not to be defined in terms of doctrine; they are common to all worship, and as conveyed in music it is in their technical exteriors only that they differ. The truth of this is amply illustrated by the best music of both faiths and most clearly, perhaps, in the music of confidence. Impressive examples are Palestrina's "Exultate Deo" and Bach's "To Thee Alone Be Glory," compositions which, though widely different in technique, are completely in agreement in their attitude. There is no question but that the music in each case means exactly what its text says, and that both have a common objective. In the Palestrina it is man who "jubilates," and it is God who is "our help." In the Bach it is the "Christian people" who sing with "hearts and voices," while it is God's "glory" that is the object of their praise. Considered as technique, the modern Protestant fashion of depicting confidence realistically differs, as might be expected, from the technique suggested by the gentler moods in its employment of a more decided, energetic type of music embodying strongly marked rhythms, bolder melody, dependence on harmony, and especially in its rejection of enervating and emotional chromatics. Confidence, as expressed by the older composers and by the moderns, is illustrated by the "Credo" from Palestrina's *Missa brevis* and the anthem "O Love That Wilt Not Let Me Go" by R. H. Miles. Again it is the question of balance between the human and the divine, and no reference to an analytical table of technical elements is necessary to determine how much of the secular is contained in each of the selections. Two further examples of the manner in which composers of our own time have met the problem of setting the religious literature of confidence are "Trust in Him" by Bernard Hamblen and "I Will Sing of Thy Power" by Sir Arthur Sullivan.

All technical factors aside, the music of confidence joins with the music of humility in expressing itself through all the resources of musical reality as the layman conceives of it: in an idiom that is commonplace and often out-and-out banal, in the well-worn clichés, the repetitious sequences, the inevitable melodies, and the whole foreseeable parade of secular devices that we characterize as "familiar." If God emerges but dimly from so much modern church music, it is not always the text to which the music is set that is to blame, it is the composer who will not paint in tones a picture of God that suggests anything other than man himself; and in no area of the music of confidence is this truer than in that which sets forth the ideals of the church militant. Hymn and anthem texts are full of such phrases as "God's glory," "the mighty King," "the Lord triumphant," and these, cast in terms of musical reality, point clearly in one direction, namely toward the idea of God as an aggressive, militaristic figure. If God is to be real to us we will think of him in human terms, and music must play its part. To the makers of that music there is open a wide array of technical devices which leave the hearer in no doubt about the earthly origin of the idea. Adoration, petition, the gesture of humility—there are no pictorial musical means to make these real; but the music of confidence in its military phase may be anything from the innocuous oom-pah bass of the brass band in "Onward, Christian Soldiers" to a frank imitation of the warlike trumpet or the sound of sword beaten against sword. "Lead On, O King Eternal" by Robert Terry and the plainsong "Vexilla Regis," similar to one another in subject but quite different in musical treatment, are provocative examples.

Whether or not the language of music ever could suggest the majesty of God is a matter of opinion. If that majesty is not of this earth, if God is not to be represented to us as the generalissimo of celestial armies equipped for modern warfare, or as a genial Rotarian figure exuding a kind of universal good will, then the composer needs special qualifications which in all the history of music have been rarely met. Bach had them and displayed them when, in the *Passion According to St. Matthew*, he set those three immortal measures to the words "Truly this was the Son of God." But the problem reaches the maximum of difficulty for the composer when he undertakes a musical interpretation of God's own words. If there are few notable examples of music great enough to suggest a God who is more than just one among us, there are still fewer that ring true as conveyances of actual divine utterance; works which both in text and in music come near to breaking our ties with earth. A composition which fulfills all that Canon Douglas meant by the words "God-centred" is Byrd's "I Will Not Leave You Comfortless." Here words and music are so closely united in a suggestion of the divine that for once, at least, the ideal balance is struck.

Another type of composition that invites forgetfulness of this world's immediate concerns is represented by the none too large body of "nature" hymns, such as "The Spacious Firmament on High" or the hymn which begins

> Praise the Lord, ye heavens, adore him;
> Praise him, angels in the height;
> Sun and moon, rejoice before him;
> Praise him, all ye stars and light.

Only one corner of the literature of confidence is occupied by hymns embodying thoughts of the natural universe, but these constitute a healthy presence because for the moment they do take the worshiper's mind off himself. The churchgoer can feel quite objective toward the solar system; it is so far away and so inevitable as to have little contact with reality. Therefore he finds greater comfort in texts like

> Lord, with glowing heart I'd praise Thee,
> For the bliss Thy love bestows,
> For the pard'ning grace that saves me,
> And the peace that from it flows.

I fear that I have tiresomely labored the point that the good intentions of the poet are often nullified by the modern composer to a point where through the reality, the familiarity of the musical substance, God becomes a minor figure. This has been true alike of the music of humility and the music of confidence, but at this point I should like to turn attention particularly to the poet, seizing on some lines from a hymn that was dear to our fathers and using it as provocation for the further pursuit of this study of the dominance of the human element in worship music. Here is the passage:

> I'm the child of a King! The child of a King!
> With Jesus my Saviour, I'm the child of a King!

That phrase, it seems to me, is the *leit motif* which ran through much of the Protestant thinking of the nineteenth century and which found ample voice in congregational song. Membership in the Divine Royal Family was not quite an accident of birth; it followed as an automatic consequent of some crucial act of self-dedication or upon some declaration involving agreement with precise doctrinal commitments. Come what may, one was saved for eternity. Furthermore, as the child of a King the singer was, of course, in the line of succession to the throne itself, and the full implications of that somewhat startling idea have culminated in our time in a theological statement setting up for music a very neat and as yet unsolved problem.

In the concise resolution of human doubt about the singer's ultimate destination there was, perhaps, a reaction

against the older uncertainty which accompanied the lifelong struggle to achieve perfection as personified in God.
That that emulation was not forgotten is evident in many
hymns, but the object of the striving is often frankly
stated to be not a more God-like man but a concrete
reward.

What might be called this *quid pro quo* element in the
religious attitude is openly expressed in hymns like the
one which begins:

> We come to thee, dear Saviour,
> Just because we need thee so.

But having come, and being "saved," we have nothing
more to fear; in a sense we are already of another world,
and we may as far as possible ignore the vicissitudes of
this one. Now this is what is called, if I am not mistaken,
"flight from reality," and the literature which grew up
around that precept resulted in a curious phenomenon,
for it produced the most realistic music the Christian
Church has known. Take, for example, this familiar hymn,
one verse of which I quote:

> Safe in the arms of Jesus, safe on his gentle breast;
> There by his love o'er-shaded, sweetly my soul shall rest.
> Hark, 'tis the voice of angels, borne in a song to me,
> Over the fields of glory, over the jasper sea.

No utterance could be more personal or self-centered than
that, and the only music that could properly partner it
would be music equally personal in character. Now although the standard church hymnals contained a wealth of
music sufficiently introspective to suit almost any occasion,
there was, apparently, nothing real enough to suit the
purpose here. Therefore, some new type of music had to
be found. If the prophets of the flight from reality had
had a better musical and literary background, they might
have heralded a new and glorious day for church music;

what they brought forth, however, was that embarrassingly autobiographical record of Christian snobbery, the gospel hymn. Yet that form commands my respect far more than do numbers of hymns sanctified by inclusion in our parish hymnals, for gospel hymns are just what they pretend to be. They don't talk about God in the smug musical phrases of the drawing-room ballad or the make-believe devoutness that is really the ogling sentimentality of the love song. They ignore God, just as do many of the texts they accompany.

Made up of technical formulas so common and so apparently instinctive to our nature that they constitute a kind of original musical sin within us, gospel hymns, as well as many "legitimate" hymns, are written in a sadly depreciated musical currency; in a language compounded of sentimentality and musical triteness, familiar, friendly, natural, orienting us solidly in the weekday world of musical experience. While we cannot admire this music, we can pity it as we would pity any creature forever destined to play a part for which, by nature, he was not intended. Almost any examination of text and music is bound to reveal a serious mismating. These tunes, these low-class earthy fellows, are married to the wrong girls. Some of our musical friends have a roving eye; some are frustrated comedians; while others are plain tavern-minded; but all are wed to firm-handed and pious literary ladies who know how to keep them in their place. If, for example, you are a placid and normally cheerful tune it must be difficult to be your smiling self if your wife is constantly at your elbow with the depressing query, "Shall We Gather at the River?" Or let us say that a tidy creation of Ogden Nash goes strolling by the window and our tune's eye lights up with an appreciative gleam. He knows, and we know, that it is with her that he rightfully belongs; but when his partner insists at the beginning of every verse that she will need him every hour, he isn't going to find time to brush even the fringes of indiscretion. Without meaning to strain an already aggravated domestic situation, I occasionally find myself encouraging some gospel hymn to have his fling. They're not likely to have much of a sense of loyalty, these tunes, and they fall an easy prey to the wiles of any secular text that suits them nicely. So it is that more than once in the middle of "Let the Lower Lights Be Burning" I have been embarrassed and shocked to find that what I was really doing was "Seeing Nellie Home." I would feel better if this sort of thing could be done openly, and once, being convinced of the true destiny of a Sunday School pamphlet tune, I tried unsuccessfully to get permission to issue it as a college football song. Gospel hymns represent, as I have said, connubial misfits, and this is undoubtedly one of the reasons why time has to a great extent expunged them. They still hold a nostalgic place in the affections of a vanishing generation, but in the services of enlightened churches they are never heard.

The proved accomplishments of the gospel hymn were three: it demonstrated the complete absence of any corporate sense of humor from the laity of the Protestant Church; it set in motion a flood of congregational vocal effort that up to that time had been as inarticulate as the waters of the Dead Sea; and it revealed the appalling depths to which American public musical taste could descend when left to express itself without restraint under ecclesiastical auspices. The archetype is, perhaps, "When the Roll Is Called Up Yonder I'll Be There." Mark Twain, in *A Tramp Abroad*, describes a performance of that pianistic warhorse of a generation ago, the "Battle of Prague," given by a young lady amateur in the parlor of a Swiss hotel. "None of us like mediocrity," he wrote, "but we all reverence perfection. This girl's music was perfection in its way; it was the worst music that had ever been achieved on our planet by a mere human being. . . She got an amount of anguish into the cries of the wounded that shed a new light on human suffering."[4] In the same way it may be said that gospel hymns were literal revelations of the Christian's capacity for pious self-congratulation. The man who sings "When the Roll Is Called Up Yonder" testifies that his major obligations to himself are satisfied. But as a Christian he *must*, naturally, think of his fellow men. "Faith" and "hope" are present and accounted for, but there remains "charity"; good works in general and, specifically, contributions to the organized and efficient agencies of social service, and to missions.

The question which concerns us is what becomes of music on Sunday in a service of worship which tends to make ethics an end in itself. Music is first and last an art, and sometimes a very wilful one. "If you wish me," says music, "to have a significant part in your religious celebrations, you must make of them something to which I may appropriately contribute. I am, to be sure, numbers and overtones and symbols on a printed page, but that is only the factual part of me. My real self is beauty, born of pure imagination. When I live in sound I may even take on something of the quality of God, for I am of time, but not of space, and no one has ever revealed the secret of my beauty."

> We shall do so much in the years to come, but what
>   have we done today?
> We shall give our gold in a princely sum, but what
>   did we give today?
> We shall lift the heart and dry the tear, we shall
>   plant a hope in the place of fear,
> We shall speak the words of love and cheer, but what
>   have we done today?

---

[4] *A Tramp Abroad* (Stormfield ed.; New York and London: Harper and Brothers, 1929), p. 30.

The sort of music suggested by this type of spiritual census taking I leave to your imagination. Of music as a conveyance of ethical ideas generally, it may be said that however admirable the literature of the social gospel and of personal piety, it has generated relatively little music of artistic worth. I cannot claim to know more than a comparatively small segment of the world's sacred music, but of what is really great that I do know, by far the larger part, judged by objective artistic standards, was inspired by texts which speak of God or which speak in the words of God, which treat of the miracle of the redemption of the world by Christ's death on the cross, of the supernatural, and of that which by its remoteness and its unreality is imaginatively stimulating.

This raises at once, of course, the question as to what is available by way of music for those communions which do not subscribe to "orthodox" theology. For liberal parishes which maintain a high musical standard and which respect the undeniable integrity of a vocal piece in its original form—that is, where no substitute text has been supplied—the answer has been found in a symbolic interpretation of language which, taken literally, would be contrary to belief. Other more realistically minded churches will sometimes go as far as to accept a kind of symbolism that is for the eye primarily; traditional ecclesiastical fittings which, when taken at their face value, have a definite theological significance but when interpreted symbolically represent, shall we say, the Christian virtues. These churches, however, unlike those mentioned above, refuse to accept language as a symbol and so insist on the substitution of texts more friendly to liberal thought. Text substitution is a delicate but by no means an insuperable task. Granting the ideal union that so often exists between words and a truly inspired setting of them, there is no reason why, provided the music is not changed in any slightest particular and the substitute text is appropriate to that music, another set of words should not be used. Our feelings about a text and its music are governed largely by association. Composers themselves have not hesitated to employ the same music for different sets of words, and if the traditional combination is unfamiliar, no incongruity is perceived. However, anyone attempting to replace an original text by a substitute needs, first, a sound sense of literary values and, second, the courage to resist the temptation to tamper with the music in order to fit in a rhythmically recalcitrant line. The whole process involves a compromise at best, but better this, perhaps, than the rejection of a truly fine piece of music.

Most difficult of all such problems, and the one to which earlier in this chapter I referred as still unsolved, is the selection of music to accompany services from which God, in the traditional Christian sense, is absent. It may be said at once that if my belief that there are two categories of music, one sacred and the other secular, is a valid belief, then in one sense I am not bound here to give any consideration to the music of religious humanism, because we are explicitly told that for the humanist the barriers between the sacred and the secular have been broken down.[5]

"*Seventh:* Religion consists of those actions, purposes, and experiences which are humanly significant. Nothing human is alien to the religious. It includes labor, art, science, philosophy, love, friendship, recreation—all that is in its degree expressive of intelligently satisfying human living. The distinction between the sacred and the secular can no longer be maintained.

"*Eighth:* Religious humanism considers the complete realization of human personality to be the end of man's life and seeks its development and fulfillment in the here and now. This is the explanation of the humanist's social passion.

"*Ninth:* In the place of the old attitudes involved in worship and prayer the humanist finds his religious emotions expressed in a heightened

---

[5] Articles 7, 8, 9, and 10 of "A Humanist Manifesto," *The Humanist*, May–June 1933, pp. 2–3:

sense of personal life and in a coöperative effort to promote social well-being.

"*Tenth:* It follows that there will be no uniquely religious emotions and attitudes of the kind hitherto associated with belief in the supernatural."

The inspirational possibilities of the theme of human brotherhood were once magnificently exploited through the poetry of Schiller and the music of Beethoven, but it was first of all Schiller's imagination that set alight the flame of Beethoven's genius, and we may wonder how long it will be before there will be a like partnership with like results. The word "imagination" does not occur with monotonous insistence in humanist writings, and if it is true, as I lately suggested, that the noblest examples of church music have been inspired by those imponderable matters which quicken imagination, then unless extensive borrowing be resorted to the outlook for humanist music is not encouraging. The fitting of humanist texts to borrowed music is a project requiring the highest degree of insight both literary and musical. It is a question whether musically literate worshipers will accept an ethical interpretation of a part of the Church of England Prayer Book to Palestrina's *Missa brevis*, or a badly tortured version of the music of "A Mighty Fortress Is Our God" set to a text which honors the spirit of man as the world's fairest possession, which glorifies human achievement, and which praises man's promise of still higher accomplishment.

In the earlier years of a religious movement full attention must, of course, be given to reconciling differences in viewpoint and to formulating and writing down fundamental articles of belief. But thereafter the question arises as to how, in the public affirmation of religious conviction, the unrelieved statement of ethical and doctrinal principles can be made more effective. The import of words—sometimes poetically expressed—will be understood and, perhaps, accepted, but the spirit remains not fully satisfied,

and it is here that art, and music in particular, are called
upon to play their part. In a recent article James L. Jarrett,
after speaking of the part which is played by ethics in the
program of religious humanism, asks the question whether
something more is not needed:

One part of this extra-ethical something might be called *aesthetic*,
but for fear of the front-pew reader who calls out, "Amen! More
and better hymns! Finer churches! New vestments for the choir!"
For that isn't to the point, or only to a minor portion of the point.
No, what we would like to adumbrate is a set of attitudes toward
the universe that have received *some* of their completest realiza-
tions in great works of art, and in this respect at least, merit the tag,
"Aesthetic." It is notoriously difficult to talk anything but gib-
berish about the non-musical meanings of music, but even in
eschewing the task of explaining great compositions one may hold
fast to the belief that they represent certain profound emotionalized
attitudes toward the cosmos. Without being able to translate into
concepts the "meanings" of music, many persons sensitive to the art
will not be denied their feeling that the wondrous sounds are more
than that, that they have vectors, referents. . . Whether or not the
directly designatable subject matter of works of art is religious, in
the sense of having to do with the lives of saints and the stories of
the Bible, is of little relevance to the present attempt to suggest
that in the arts there is much of a thickening substance for Humanism.[6]

These words represent a challenge, but they also serve
to remind us that although the "Humanist Manifesto," issued in 1933, paid its respects to art as a factor in religion,
the humanist church has made little progress in its approach
to an ideal of beauty. The problem for the humanists is
admittedly a difficult one, but almost everywhere in Protestantism are to be found luminous negative examples for
their guidance, and it is to be hoped that very soon religious humanism as a whole, rather than the individual
clergyman and layman, will deal thoughtfully with this

---

[6] "Must Religious Humanism Be Thin?" *The Humanist*, May–June
1950, pp. 109, 110.

matter and will attempt, at least, to establish a musical policy and practice set at the highest artistic plane.

The material of this book has been predicated on the assumption that the terms "sacred music" and "secular music" do not mean the same thing, and further, that the term "sacred music" requires a more specific definition than that it is set to religious words or performed under ecclesiastical circumstances. The thesis persistently advanced is that while there is nothing intrinsically sacred or secular in any piece of music, its classification must first be determined by the nature of its technical substance. In my second chapter I attempted to isolate several technical elements, identifying, on the basis of association, some as logical material for worship music and others as especially fitted for the service of the world; and it was pointed out that music from which rhythmic activity, chromaticism, tunefulness, and extensive dissonance were absent demonstrated how the eloquent manipulation of technical resource could result in a type of music so remote from any suggestion of the secular as to make it the normal conveyance of the ideas contained in sacred poetry and the ideal agent for setting up the detached, unworldly atmosphere appropriate to divine worship. In a great deal of that music the human element was represented by hardly more than a gesture; but with the coming of the Reformation there appeared signs of change. Attention became focussed on the individual, and eventually church music became the individual's immediate concern, with the result that in our time the worshiper asks that music shall keep pace with his demand that it shall exert a moral uplift on the erring; create a reassuring atmosphere of spirituality for those safely within the fold; invest the poetic expression of religious sentiments with a comfortable and familiar earthiness which should help to make worship a function in which the practical, everyday sort of Christian may

take part without a consciousness of make-believe; afford
him on Sunday an experience which may yield pleasure
and which at least will not disturb by its strangeness; fill
in the chinks of the badly coördinated Protestant service;
muffle the sound of coins as they drop into the collection
plate; fold up its wings and plod along beside versified
treatises on social theory; and finally interpret everything,
even Paradise, in terms of everyday, mundane experience—
each of these demands imposing on music a language in
which the accent is less and less on God and more and
more on man, until finally and actually God, as in religious
humanism, is no longer a factor to be reckoned with.
Certainly beyond this point the humanization of church
music may be pursued no further. Whether it be the
music of humility or the music of confidence, ultimate
reality, as the very human eyes of the worshiper see it, is
achieved.

VI

Church Music and Imagination

Just as many of the good features of our church music have grown out of religious and musical idealism, so most of the curious manifestations of artistic short-sightedness observable in our choice and administration of worship music are the product of faulty education. I do not mean that church music, both Catholic and Protestant, is what it is because the layman has not profited by an intensive training in all branches of music; indeed, I am inclined to think that if we could suppress most elementary public school music education for twenty years not only church music but all music in this country might benefit. The trouble is not with any single branch of teaching; it infests the whole of education today, and it comes from neglect of the one element without which all human sense remains shackled to things not as they are, but as they *seem* to be. I refer to the element of imagination, a word which has frequently appeared on these pages.

I do not know whether the reader is acquainted with the Baxters. They originated in the mind of a cartoonist named Crockett Johnson, whose whimsical genius and enlightened humor have added immeasurably to the fund of human happiness. The Baxters represent the great literal-minded American public. Their little boy Barnaby has a playmate, Jane, and both children appear to their parents, one may imagine, as perfectly normal children, until one night a pixie with pink wings, and an enormous black cigar which doubles as a magic wand, flies in through Barnaby's window and installs himself as Barnaby's fairy godfather. Thereafter, Barnaby's world and Jane's too revolves about this extraordinary little creature who calls himself by the quite unfairylike name of Mr. J. J. O'Malley. There are gnomes, leprechauns, and elves, all of whom play an active part in this fantastic narrative, to say nothing of Gorgon, Barnaby's dog, who, as one might expect, can carry on rational and often provocative conversations with the other participants—that is, all except Mr. and Mrs. Baxter to whom, naturally, a dog is a dog. Mr. and Mrs. Baxter always just miss seeing Mr. O'Malley as he passes behind them through the room; and even if they did see him, they would never believe it but would promptly mount the stairs in search of some orthodox offset to the type of temporary digestive disorder that produces visual distortions of a terrifying nature.

When Mr. O'Malley works a miracle such as that of giving Mrs. Baxter's house a thorough cleaning from top to bottom in Mrs. Baxter's absence, that lady, although the charwoman may declare on oath that she has not been near the premises, will find some natural explanation of the occurence that is twice as improbable as Barnaby's simple declaration that it is the work of his fairy godfather. You do not, of course, either expect or want Mr. and Mrs. Baxter to believe in the existence of Mr. O'Malley; indeed, we hold our breath whenever the little pixie passes the window for fear they *will* see him and thus reduce him to the sphere of grown-up reality where he would be no more the pompous, unpredictable, fascinating little gentle-man with pink wings, but a plain, deflated *reductio ad absurdum*. No, Mr. O'Malley is the exclusive possession of childhood, and the story, as we follow it, is utterly diverting and original. For me, however, the fantasy and the humor are of secondary importance. Barnaby's true significance, I believe, lies in the lesson which unintentionally perhaps he teaches; a lesson that so needs to be dinned into American ears that I would make Barnaby required reading for every teacher of little children, and for every parent-teacher association as well. For Mr. and Mrs. Baxter are symbols; symbols of that incredible stupidity which refuses to admit or to encourage in children the one faculty in which they are supreme, the faculty of imagination. In a way, I am profoundly sorry for Mr. and Mrs. Baxter. They were, perhaps, brought up in homes where childish flights of fancy were drastically repressed, and where imaginative exuberance in the interpretation of plain facts was viewed with dismay and taken to be the sure prophecy of adult criminality. The Baxters may have forgotten that as children they were heirs of that dearest common heritage of childhood, the capacity to create and to live in a world beyond their senses. That we can forgive them; but to try in every way from argument to psychiatry to destroy for Barnaby his belief in the actual existence of Mr. O'Malley, that, I say, is indefensible, cruel, and in the truest sense against nature. Mr. Baxter (who, I am sure, is chairman of his parish music committee), smoking his pipe, practical, self-assured, and convinced beyond the shadow of a doubt that the world is exactly what it seems to be and nothing more, says to Mrs. Baxter, "It's not because Barnaby *dreams* he has a Fairy Godfather. I'm worried because he won't admit it's only a dream." And with that pronouncement Mr. Baxter establishes himself as the symbol and patron saint of the American home, the American school, the American newspaper, and the American Protestant Church.

Where in education is imagination given even reasonably free play? Like church music, education must be *real;* it must prove its value by submitting to measurement

and tabulation, and the final test of its worth is whether
in the estimation of experts it fulfills the categorical requirements laid down for it; in short, whether or not it
works. We begin by assuming that what a child cannot
understand is unproductive educational material. So we
do not read real literature to him, because we cannot
believe that what he does not intellectually apprehend
can possibly impress him or do him good. We have forgotten that when we were children it was the incomprehensible and mysteriously suggestive passages from the
Scriptures that used to fascinate us, that we used to mis-
pronounce and wonder about. We overlook the myth and
the folk tale, perennial incitements to childish fancy, and
give a boy books about Johnny-next-door and the work-
ings of the United States Post Office or the internal com-
bustion engine. And when we get around to introducing
him to Virgil and Shakespeare we present them as two
pestilential grammarians who wrote for the sole purpose
of creating vexing rhetorical problems.

Music, of all subjects, offers the greatest opportunity
for the training of the imagination. In the truest sense you
cannot teach a small child music, you can only expose
him to it, and therefore the most beneficial method is to
leave him alone with it; to give him beautiful songs to
sing; to allow the unexplainable magic that resides in even
a single folk melody to work its will without interference.
But that is not education, we are told. The child must be
hurried on to the factual and arithmetical phases of music;
hardly is the sound of music familiar to him before he must
be set to reading symbols and counting rhythms, with the
result that music becomes for him not a stimulating and an
imaginative pursuit but a distasteful discipline. If we play
him records, then out of the imagined omniscience of our
grown-up point of view we put before him music which
we think will interest and amuse him; not the gay and

rhythmically propulsive music of Haydn and Mozart, or even that of moderns like Stravinsky, which children do love and which may evoke physical interpretation, but music with a story or with words, which confines them to the routine and the familiar.[1] Even at a later age we cannot trust a child to use his imagination, if indeed by this time the imaginative faculty, at least as far as music is concerned, is not atrophied. We acquaint him with a piece of pure instrumental music which we feel obliged to reinforce with some "meaning." It represents an automobile in motion, or children playing tag, or we connect it with a story that will furnish an interest which we cannot believe music to possess unaided by exterior props.

This limitation of the educational process to what is real, measurable, and experiential is not new. Generations in this country have suffered from it, with the result that we are literally a nation on crutches. Not only must the newspaper picture have its arrow or its cross which marks the spot, but it must have as well its explanatory sentence to tell us the purpose of the arrow or the cross. On one of those rare occasions when the radio invaded the realm of fantasy, on the mistaken assumption that the preposterously improbable nature of the material could not fail to label it as pure fiction, the country, having no imaginative resource, took the broadcast seriously; panics resulted, and some persons were terrified almost to the point of attempting suicide. The soundless and talkless moving pictures were one of the last outposts to fall in the war to make the world safe for popular mental stagnation. In these times any mention of death must be accompanied by a musical effect which is the sublimation of a thousand funerals. If the interior of a house is shown replete with

---

[1] *New York Sunday Times* of December 10, 1950, lists " 'The Men Who Come to Our House' (2–6 age group)" which "describes the milkman and the others (ending with Daddy) ... "

all the pageantry of mourning, it is not enough. So you are shown the front door with a wreath so preternaturally large that its meaning could not possibly escape the most wayfaring of observers. And now, God help us, there is television which of all the weapons designed by science to annihilate every provocation to the use of our already neglected imaginations is the most lethal.

For those who watched with dismay the increase in public mental spoon-feeding, there was still one reassurance. However flat and unimaginative the modern service of worship may have been, how full the music, language, and surroundings of thinly disguised intruders from the outside world, one could count on it that for perhaps five minutes each week the worshiper would find himself in a sphere of beauty, transported thither by the magic of the poetry of the King James version. It was inevitable, I suppose, that sooner or later the lovers of the commonplace, in religion as in all things, should be driven to lay violent hands on it. Preceded by extended and lucid detail which clearly frames the picture, the import of the words "Lazarus, come forth" ought not to prove elusive. If it does, you may turn to a modern version which renders it "Lazarus, come out." For my part, I do not want to know the exact dimensions of the New Jerusalem in the Book of Revelation. Cubits and furlongs are just the right words, for, not knowing precisely what they mean, I get from their sound a vague sense of vastness and unreality. But if you want to compare your city with Heaven, the modern translator has given you the figures for the latter in miles and even in yards. If we continue in this direction the next generation of worshipers will be so imaginatively enfeebled that we will have to reinforce Sunday's reading of the story of the Creation or the collapse of the walls of Jericho by television and sound effects. In many a Protestant service, the rhythmic sweep and poetic imagery of the older version represent the sole concession to beauty in an otherwise literal-minded order of exercises, and even this the prophets of reality would destroy.

G. R. Elliott, speaking of the alliance between Renaissance naturalism and sentimental humanitarianism, refers to "the poetic decline of the Christian Church" as a "parallel . . . phenomenon."

Religion is (like nothing else) greater than poetry, but its long history has shown over and over again that religion (like everything else) is bound to crumble when it is poetically inadequate; that is, when its poetry . . . is too meagre or too cheap. One way of expressing the supremacy of Christianity is to say that it and it alone is, in its most catholic aspect, entirely adequate poetically. But just for that reason the narrowing and stiffening of the Christian imagination during the post-Reformation era, both in the Catholic and in the Protestant branches of the Church, was extraordinarily disastrous.[2]

It is this heritage, then, that has so materially contributed to the undoing of our ecclesiastical art. Beauty, mystery, religion, music; the thread which runs through all these words, the element which they possess in common, is *imagination*. When education wakes up to the fact that a love of beauty and a respect for its significance are important, our church music will begin to improve on many fronts. As Alfred North Whitehead declares:

The ultimate motive power, alike in science, in morality, and in religion, is the sense of value, the sense of importance. It takes the various forms of wonder, of curiosity, of reverence, of worship, of tumultuous desire for merging personality in something beyond itself. This sense of value imposes on life incredible labours, and apart from it life sinks back into the passivity of its lower types. The most penetrating exhibition of this force is the sense of beauty, the aesthetic sense of realized perfection. This thought leads me to

---

[2] *Humanism and Imagination* (Chapel Hill: University of North Carolina Press, 1938), p. 19.

ask, whether in our modern education we emphasize sufficiently the functions of art.[3]

It is from the kindergartens and from the primary schools of today that the laymen, clergy, and musicians of tomorrow will come, and unless in every department of education we face squarely this imaginative deficiency, this slighting of beauty as a resource of life, religion and worship will continue to lack for the great majority of Protestants those inborn characteristics which would, if we would but permit them, make of the Sunday service and its music something profoundly and in its *true* sense, "real." For beauty, whether you interpret it in terms of morality, or God, or nature, is the ultimate reality.

There is, I am convinced, but one logical purpose for which church music may be employed, and that is to the glory of God; not for any of the psychological, social, opportunistic, or utilitarian ends for which our worship music is now tortured out of its true nature, but as an offering, a sacrifice, a return in kind of God's gift of beauty to man. The finest church music suggests the church and nothing outside of it, for that music is not sensuous or emotional as is the music of our secular world; it is merely an eloquent yet inconspicuous reinforcement of the ideas embodied in the text it accompanies. The perception of this fact depends not at all on a technical knowledge of music. One need but ask himself, "Is this the music of my everyday world? Is its language familiar to me in many forms? Although I have not heard this particular selection before, is it made up of the constituents common to most of the music I am accustomed to hear? Would it serve equally well as the setting for an anthem and for a text secular in character? Or is it a speech

[3] *The Aims of Education and Other Essays* (New York: The Macmillan Co., 1929), pp. 62, 63.

apart; remote, archaic perhaps, sacerdotal, strange; a language to which the church alone would be hospitable?"

A professor at St. Andrews University, speaking once of Iona in Scotland, described that island, in its unbelievable and unearthly beauty, as "one of the thin places where the other world shows through." That is exactly what I feel about the greatest monuments of the music of the Christian church—that there is something of another world in them—and for that reason, perhaps, we too readily dismiss them as beyond our ken. Little of such music is familiar to most of our choirs; its rareness is, incidentally, one of its unmistakable marks of identification. There is not the least danger of its losing its sacred associations by undue exploitation on the radio; it will not offer itself as grateful material for domestic music-making about the piano; I do not expect that the organ grinder who occasionally visits the Harvard Yard will substitute it for his inevitable and increasingly asthmatic rendering of "What a Friend We Have in Jesus."

Our generation is an individualistic and, above all, a realistic one, and I see no prospect of extensive improvement in church music either Roman Catholic or Protestant until by purging it of its worldly substance we make of it something that is uniquely the music of worship.

Appendix

A Selected List of Anthems

Index

Mass in D N.3

Kyrie

Haydn

Missa solennis

Kyrie
Andante solenne

Franz Liszt

The following list of anthems is in no sense a comprehensive catalogue. It represents a selection of pieces chosen to exemplify the principles set forth in the previous pages.

Every item has been published in multiple copies obtainable from music dealers. A piece having two texts is listed under its English title. Mention should be made of Concord Anthem Books 1 and 2 published by the E. C. Schirmer Music Company of 221 Columbus Avenue, Boston, Massachusetts. Although a majority of the pieces in those collections have been published separately, their titles, which might properly appear in this list, are not included.

The publishers are given in their short-title form in parentheses following the titles of the anthems:

Aug	Augener	JF	J. Fischer
BMC	Boston Music Co.	MP	Music Press
CF	Carl Fischer	Nov	Novello
ECS	E. C. Schirmer	OD	Oliver Ditson
GS	G. Schirmer	OUP	Oxford University Press
HWG	H. W. Gray	RDR	R. D. Rowe
JC	J. Curwen	S&B	Stainer and Bell

A Selected List of Anthems

BACH, J. S.   *Voices:* SATB
Chorales, ed. by Clough-
Leighter, Bks. I, II, III (ECS).
Acc: Yes. *Text:* English.

BLOW   *Voices:* SATB
Put me not to rebuke (OUP).
Acc: No. *Text:* English.

BRAHMS   *Voices:* SAATBB
Grant unto me the joy of Thy
salvation (GS). *Acc:* No.
Text: German and English.

Voices: SATB
O Savior, throw the heavens
wide (GS). *Acc:* No. *Text:*
German and English.

BYRD   *Voices:* SATB
Arise, shine forth in splendor
(Nov). *Acc:* No. *Text:* Latin
and English.

Voices: SATB
Day of sanctification
(HWG). *Acc:* No. *Text:*
Latin and English.

Voices: SATB
Hail, O hail, true body
(OUP). *Acc:* No. *Text:* Latin
and English.

Voices: SSATB
I will not leave you comfort-
less (ECS). *Acc:* No. *Text:*
English.

BYRD   *Voices:* SAT
Lord hear my prayer (S&B).*
Acc: No. *Text:* English.

Voices: SAT
Lord, in Thy rage (S&B).*
Acc: No. *Text:* English.

Voices: SAB
Lord, in Thy wrath (S&B).*
Acc: No. *Text:* English.

Voices: SAT
O God, which art most merci-
ful (S&B).* *Acc:* No. *Text:*
English.

Voices: SSATBB
Praise our Lord all ye gentiles
(S&B). *Acc:* No. *Text:* Eng-
lish.

Voices: SAATB
Prevent us, O Lord (OUP).
Acc: No. *Text:* English.

Voices: SAT
Right blest are they (S&B).*
Acc: No. *Text:* English.

Voices: SSATB
The souls of the righteous
(HWG). *Acc:* No. *Text:*
Latin and English.

Voices: SATB
Then did priests make offer-
ing (OUP). *Acc:* No. *Text:*
Latin and English.

---

* The Byrd titles marked with an asterisk are also published by S&B
in a transposed edition for ATB.

FARRANT   *Voices:* SATB
Call to remembrance, O Lord
(GS). *Acc:* Yes. *Text:* English.

FRANCK, C.   *Voices:* SATB
They are ever blessed (ECS).
Acc: Yes. *Text:* English.

GIBBONS   *Voices:* SATB
Blessed be the Lord (Nov).
Acc: No. *Text:* English.

    Voices: SSAATB
Hosanna to the son of David
(OUP). *Acc:* No. *Text:* English.

    Voices: SAATB
O Thou, the central orb
(ECS). *Acc:* Yes. *Text:* English.

GRETCHANINOFF   *Voices:* SATB
O praise the name of the Lord
(JF). *Acc:* No. *Text:* English.
    Voices: SATB
Praise the Lord, O my soul
(HWG). *Acc:* No. *Text:* English.

    Voices: SATB
The Cherubic Hymn
(HWG). *Acc:* No. *Text:* English.

HANDL   *Voices:* SATB
Behold, how doth the righteous man perish (ECS). *Acc:* No. *Text:* Latin and English.
    Voices: SATB
O blessed are ye (RDR). *Acc:* No. *Text:* Latin and English.

HOLST   *Voices:* SATB
Psalm CXLVIII (Aug). *Acc:* No. *Text:* English.

HOLST   *Voices:* SATB
Turn back O man (S&B).
Acc: Yes. *Text:* English.

LASSUS   *Voices:* SATB
Lord, to Thee we turn (ECS).
Acc: No. *Text:* English.

    Three equal voices
Three Psalms (MP). *Acc:* No. *Text:* German and English.

    Two equal voices
Twelve Motets (MP). *Acc:* No. *Text:* Latin.

MORALES   *Voices:* SATTB
Let us thoroughly amend
(OD). *Acc:* No. *Text:* Latin and English.

NIKOLSKI   *Voices:* SATB
Praise ye the name of the Lord (BMC). *Acc:* No. *Text:* English.

PALESTRINA   *Voices:* SATB
Many tongues that day were spoken (RDR). *Acc:* No. *Text:* Latin and English.

    Voices: SATB
O King of Glory (ECS). *Acc:* No. *Text:* Latin and English.

    Voices: SATB
Take my yoke upon you (GS). *Acc:* No. *Text:* Latin and English.

    Voices: SATB
Unto Thee lift I up mine eyes (ECS). *Acc:* No. *Text:* Latin and English.

PRAETORIUS   *Voices:* SATB
Be not dismayed, thou little
flock (CF). *Acc:* No. *Text:*
English.

Voices: SATB
Now is the old year passed
away (GS). *Acc:* No. *Text:*
English.

PURCELL   *Voices:* SATB
O God, Thou art my God
(Nov). *Acc:* Yes. *Text:* Eng-
lish.

Voices: SATB
O sing unto the Lord (Nov).
Acc: Yes. *Text:* English.

SCHÜTZ   *Voices:* SATB
Four Psalms (MP). *Acc:* Yes.
Text: German and English.

Two medium voices
Give ear, O Lord (MP). *Acc:*
Yes. *Text:* German and Eng-
lish.

Voices: SSAATTBB
Sing to the Lord a new song
(GS). *Acc:* No. *Text:* Eng-
lish.

SWEELINCK   *Voices:* SSATBB
Arise, oh ye servants of God
(GS). *Acc:* No. *Text:* French
and English.

Voices: SATB
O Lord God, to thee be praise
(GS). *Acc:* No. *Text:* French
and English

Voices: SATB
Psalm 96 (MP). *Acc:* No.
Text: French and English.

Voices: SATB
Psalm 102 (MP). *Acc:* No.
Text: French and English.

TALLIS   *Voices:* SATB
I heard a voice from heaven
(OUP). *Acc:* No. *Text:* Latin
and English.

Voices: SATB
O Lord, give thy holy spirit
(OUP). *Acc:* No. *Text:* Eng-
lish.

TCHAIKOVSKY   *Voices:* SATB
Cherubim Song (GS). *Acc:*
No. *Text:* English.

Voices: SATB
O praise the name of the Lord
(HWG). *Acc:* No. *Text:*
English.

THOMPSON   *Voices:* SATB
Alleluia (ECS). *Acc:* No.
Text: English.

Voices: SSAATTBB
But these are they that forsake
the Lord, from "The Peaceable Kingdom" (ECS). *Acc:*
No. *Text:* English.

Voices: SATB
The paper reeds by the
brooks, from "The Peaceable
Kingdom" (ECS). *Acc:* No.
Text: English.

TOMKINS   *Voices:* SSTB
O pray for the peace of Jeru-
salem (OUP). *Acc:* No. *Text:*
English.

Voices: SAATB
When David heard (S&B).
Acc: No. *Text:* English.

TYE   *Voices:* SATB
Praise ye the Lord (OUP).
Acc: No. *Text:* English.

Voices: SATB
Sing unto the Lord (OUP).
Acc: No. *Text:* English.

VAUGHAN WILLIAMS
Voices: SSAATTBB
Lord, Thou hast been our refuge (JC). *Acc:* Yes. *Text:* English.

Voices: SATB
Magnificat and Nunc Dimittis (JC). *Acc:* Yes. *Text:* English.

Voices: SSAATTBB
O vos omnes (JC). *Acc:* No. *Text:* Latin.

Voices: SSAATTBB
Te Deum in G (OUP). *Acc:* Yes. *Text:* English.

VICTORIA *Voices:* SATB
All ye that pass by (OD). *Acc:* No. *Text:* Latin and English.

VICTORIA *Voices:* SATB
Are ye come out as against a thief (OD). *Acc:* No. *Text:* Latin and English.

WILLAN ·*Voices:* SATB
Hail, gladdening light (HWG). *Acc:* No. *Text:* English.

Voices: SATB
Lo, in the time appointed (OUP). *Acc:* No. *Text:* English.

Voices: SATB
O King, to whom all things do live (CF). *Acc:* No. *Text:* English.

Voices: SATB
O sacred feast (HWG). *Acc:* No. *Text:* English.

Index